20 Patterns for
Santa Carvers

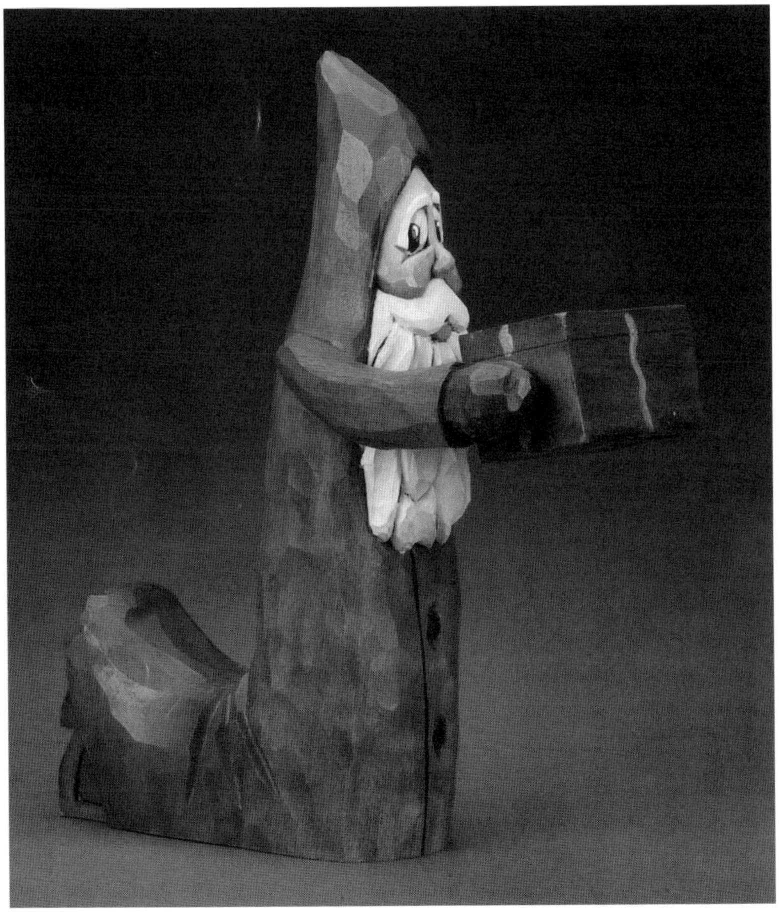

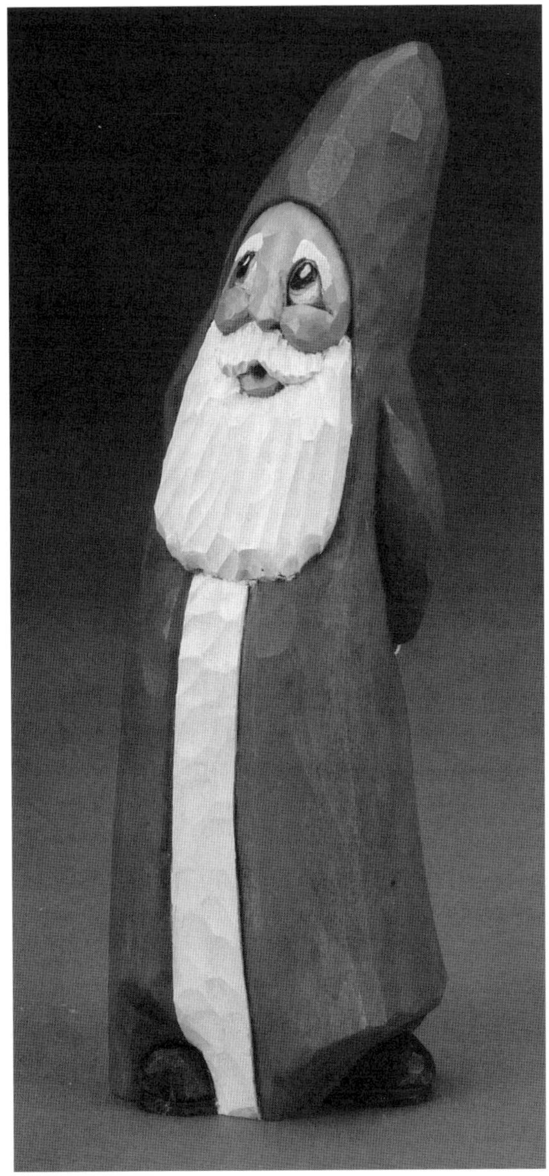

Al Streetman

Schiffer Publishing Ltd®

4880 Lower Valley Road, Atglen, PA 19310 USA

ACKNOWLEDGMENTS

The following people helped make this book possible. I thank you all.

Tim and Debbie Effrem, Woodcarvers Supply, Inc. (1-800-284-6229): For graciously providing the excellent quality tools I am using on my current projects. They carry an outstanding assortment of fine carving tools, supplies, and books.
DecoArt: The paint samples were excellent, and satisfactory in all respects.
Royal Brush Mfg.,Inc.:High quality paintbrushes at an affordable price.
David Mather, Tuckaway Timber (603-795-4534): The best basswood and white pine I have found for carving, and very reasonable prices.

CONTENTS

Library of Congress Card Number: 2003100149

Designed by Joseph M. Riggio Jr.
Type set in Korinna BT heading font/text font Korinna BT

ISBN: 0-7643-1837-3
Printed in China

Published by Schiffer Publishing Ltd.
4880 Lower Valley Road
Atglen, PA 19310
Phone: (610) 593-1777; Fax: (610) 593-2002
E-mail: Info@schifferbooks.com
Please visit our web site catalog at **www.schifferbooks.com**
We are always looking for people to write books on new and related subjects. If you have an idea for a book please contact us at the above address.

This book may be purchased from the publisher.
Include $3.95 for shipping.
Please try your bookstore first.
You may write for a free catalog.

In Europe, Schiffer books are distributed by
Bushwood Books
6 Marksbury Ave.
Kew Gardens
Surrey TW9 4JF England
Phone: 44 (0) 20 8392-8585; Fax: 44 (0) 20 8392-9876
E-mail: Bushwd@aol.com
Free postage in the U.K., Europe; air mail at cost.

INTRODUCTION

If you still haven't had your fill of Santa carving, here is another book of ideas to keep you busy. In this book we are going to carve a "windblown Santa," holding a lantern and grasping a walking stick as he tries to make his way through the storm. This is another one of my whimsical creations, which is fun to carve and has been a good seller. It offers a slight but not difficult challenge, and provides some tips and tricks for arm and hand carving, and multipart construction techniques. This method lets you make maximum use of grain direction, in order to save valuable wood from being wasted, and to make the carving easier. It was often used by the old masters hundreds of years ago, so don't let anyone tell you it's "cheating."

Some of you may observe that my carving project is not as complex or detailed as you might carve it. *There is a method to my madness*. In this book, as in my previous books, I have tried to design a project that would yield a nice result, yet not be so complex or involved that the *beginning* wood carver would not be able to accomplish it. I want to reach as many wood carvers as possible, and share the joy of carving with them. As the beginners gain more experience, they can add additional details as desired.

Except for the actual carving project, I have not included specific carving instructions. I have found that each carver has his or her own style, and each has their preference for which tool to use in a particular area, or to achieve a particular effect.

Rather than giving a vague instruction such as "use a small gouge," I have listed the particular size gouge I used in the different steps of the carving project, as we move through each step of the carving. This is more for the benefit of the beginning carver, than of the more experienced ones. If you don't have these particular sizes of gouges or tools, use something similar.

The patterns in this book include approximate dimensions of the side and front views, if you desire to carve them to the same size as I originally designed them. If you desire a larger or smaller version, simply enlarge or shrink the pattern on a photocopying machine.

As you scan through the different patterns, you will notice that some are fairly simple, and some are moderately complex. I have tried to provide enough choices to accommodate your mood. Whether you are looking for something that is quick and easy to carve, or something that will take a day or two, there should be a pattern to fit your need.

Before you begin the actual carving project, I *highly recommend* that you read through the entire book at least once. You may notice that a detail that was not completely clear to you in the carving section may become *very* clear in the painting section. Often the details show up much better, once the wood has been given some life with a coat of paint. **Remember**, if we carve it in the first part of the book, we'll paint it later, so you have at least two sections of the book for a reference. Some of the Santas in the pattern section will also show up in the gallery and study model section, so that will give you a third source for a reference.

I use Basswood whenever possible, but any soft wood such as Jelutong, clear Spruce, or Sugar/White Pine will work equally well. If possible, use a bandsaw with a 1/8" blade to cut out the side and front profiles. The bandsaw will allow you to release the rough version of the Santa from the block of wood faster than trying to use a coping saw or other means to cut out the pattern. I have been obtaining my wood from Tuckaway Timber Company (they are on the internet, if you need to reach them), and have been very pleased with its quality and price.

GENERAL NOTES

1. Trace the pattern you have decided to carve or make a copy of it on a photocopying machine. Glue the pattern you copied or traced onto some heavy paper such as poster board or a manila file folder. When the glue is dry, cut out the pattern. This method will prevent you from ruining the master patterns in your book.
2. Lay your pattern on the wood, trace the outline of it, and saw it out. *The arrows shown on the patterns with a "G" superimposed over them, indicate the recommended grain direction of the wood to obtain best results and easiest carving.*
3. You should now have a rough blank ready to be carved.
4. Use your own techniques and style to bring the carving to the finished stage.

PROJECT CARVING TOOLS

For those of you who may want to duplicate the cuts I made using the same tools as I used, I have listed below the tools used in the carving project. If you are already an experienced carver, then most likely you have some favorite tools that you prefer to use in order to achieve the desired results and effects. New carvers are sometimes overwhelmed by the variety and multitude of carving tools and accessories available in different stores and catalogs. Before you go out and take a second mortgage on the ranch just to finance all the tools you "think" you will need to get the job accomplished, try this approach: purchase a fixed-blade bench knife (fairly long wooden handle with about a 1-1/2" long blade, a couple of V-gouges (perhaps 1/8" and 1/4"), and a couple of U-gouges. Learn how to sharpen them, because they do not normally come ready to use, no matter what the catalogs may say. Dull knives and gouges are one of the leading causes of frustration for new carvers, because they haven't realized yet that the dullness of their tools is causing the problem. This is the point that some would-be great carvers give up and move on to needlepoint or something else less intimidating. There are many good books on the market that will tell you in words, and show you with photos, how to get the proper edge on the various types of knives and gouges.

Once you have learned how to put a good edge on your tools, maintaining that edge will then only require a mild stropping. You will, of course, have to put the tool on a sharpening stone occasionally, but unless you have dropped the tool or otherwise damaged the edge, most of the time a light stropping will be all that is required.

After diligently working hard to make sure your tools are sharp, create your carving then look at the effects the V-gouge and the U-gouge can create. You may even want to make some practice cuts on some scrap wood, in order to observe the various effects that can be achieved with each type of tool. Whichever one best suits your likes and is the most visually appealing to you, then that is the type to obtain more of to round out your arsenal.

I mainly use a V-gouge to outline areas where I want to remove wood and to create things such as wrinkles and soles on shoes, but personally I find that I use the U-type gouges much more frequently. Their effect on areas such as hair and beards suits me more than the effect achieved by V-gouges. You may feel that the "V" does a better job for you, and that is your right to feel that way. There is no "correct" tool to use, except the one which gives the effect that makes you the happiest. It's all a part of the personal "style" that you have, or that you will develop. I have been using tools from Wood Carver's Supply in Englewood, Florida recently. These tools are of excellent quality and priced very reasonably. If you aren't sure about which tool would be best for you, give them a call. They will work with you on the phone to ensure that you get just the right item(s).

- #39 3 mm 60 degree true V-gouge
- #39 4.5mm 60 degree true V-gouge
- #9 4.5 mm deep U-gouge
- #9 6 mm deep U-gouge
- #1 10 mm straight gouge.
- General Whittling knife, 1-1/8" blade

TIPS

1. EYES

A. **QUILT PIN METHOD:** I often use various sizes of plastic-head quilting pins to make eyes. Mark where you want the eyes to be on the finished carving. Using a drill and bit that is slightly larger than the pinhead you are going to use, make a hole for each eye.

Using wire cutters, snip off the pinhead, leaving about 1/4" of the pin attached to the head.

Insert the pinhead into the eye socket, with the pin end going in first. Use a nailset to seat the head into the hole until only a small orb protrudes. This gives a fairly realistic eye without too much effort on your part. For extra detail, remove a triangular-shaped piece of wood from the sides of the pinhead. This will make a very realistic eye when it is painted.

B. **PUNCH METHOD:** A second way to create eyes the easy way is to use carver's eye punches. Select the size eye punch you want to use, based on the size of the eye sockets you have made. Push the eye punch against the socket firmly and rotate it. After making both eyes, remove triangular-shaped pieces of wood from the corners to give more detail. Use your knife, if necessary, to smooth and round off the eyeball.

C. **FOOTBALL METHOD:** A more realistic way to make eyes is to first of all carve the eye sockets so that about a 90-degree angle is formed. Lightly sketch in a football-shaped eye in each socket, such that the top half of the football is on the upper half of the socket, and the lower half of the football is on the lower half of the socket. When you sketch in the footballs, make the outside ends lower than the inside ends. Using the tip of your knife, score the football outline to a depth of about 1/16". Now use the tip of your knife to remove triangle-shaped pieces of wood from the left and right corner of each eye. This will leave a small section of wood inside each football, which will be the eyeball. Use your knife to round off and smooth the eyeball. You can vary the way you remove the triangle-shaped corners, if you want the eyes to be looking more to one side, rather than straight ahead.

D. **MOUND METHOD:** The most realistic way to make eyes is to first rough-carve the nose so it is standing out from the face. Next, sketch a circle or oval on each side of the nose to represent where the eye mounds will be located. Using a smaller V-gouge, such as a 1/8" size, or your knife tip, go around the circles or ovals so the mounds will be defined and separated from the face area. Use your knife to round the sharp edges of the mounds, and the face area around the mounds.

Divide the mounds into thirds by sketching two curved horizontal lines across each one, making sure that the lines join at each corner of the mound. (Look at your own eyes in a mirror to see what I mean here). Using your knife tip, score each horizontal line about 1/16" deep. Working from the **center** of the eye mound, use your knife tip to shave **upward** toward the top horizontal line, and **downward** toward the bottom horizontal line. This will make the eyelids stand out from the eyeball area. Finally, remove small triangular pieces of wood from each corner of the eye, so the eyeball will be rounded from left to right, as well as top to bottom.

Changing the size and shape of the mounds, and the spacing between the horizontal lines, will allow you to achieve many effects and expressions on your carvings.

One last thing concerning eyes: Don't get upset if you discover that you have carved one eye smaller or at a different angle than the other eye. This "accident" may work to your advantage. It will lend an interesting variation to the carving, and no one has to know you didn't do it that way on purpose!!

2. BUYING WOOD

When buying wood, whether it be Basswood, Spruce, or some other type, try to pick the **lightest** pieces. They tend to have less fat and sap in them, so they are **easier** to carve.

3. WRINKLES AND FOLDS

To help determine where you want to place some wrinkles and folds in the arms, torso and legs, observe and note where the wood grain changes direction as you are carving. Usually in the crook of an elbow or behind the knees, you will notice that wood "fuzzies" try to appear, no matter how carefully you carve or how sharp your knife is. That is because the wood grain direction is changing, and in one direction or the other, you are trying to carve against the grain, thus the "fuzzies" appear. These spots are perfect candidates for wrinkles and folds, made with a large "V" tool or by cutting wedges out with your knife. As a beginning carver, if you do nothing more than add a few cuts in these areas, you will be amazed at the difference in the way the carving looks. With experience, you will start noticing other places to add wrinkles and folds, and some day you will be the best carver in the world!

4. ENLARGING PATTERNS

For those of you who have never had much practice enlarging or reducing patterns, or being able to calculate how much enlargement or reduction you need to select on the photocopying machine, here are some general guidelines:

Let's say you have a pattern that shows a side profile requiring 2" thick wood, and you want to make the pattern larger so it will fit on 3" thick wood. Use the following formula to calculate what percentage enlargement to select on the copier:

[New Dimension Desired ÷ Present Dimension] x 100 = % to select on copier machine

Using our example, this would work out as follows:

[3" ÷ 2"] x 100 = **150%**.

Going the other way, let's say you have a pattern that shows a 2" side profile, and you want to reduce it down so it will fit on a piece of 1-3/4" thick wood. Using the same formula, it works out as follows:

[1.75" ÷ 2"] x 100 = **87.5%**.

If the machine you are using won't go large enough or small enough to get the job done on the first try, additional steps may be required. Go ahead and make your first copy using the largest enlargement or reduction setting you can select. Measure the **new** dimensions on your *copy*, **(which will now be your Present Dimension**), then use the same formula as before to calculate how much additional enlargement or reduction is needed to get the pattern to the size you desired it to be.

5. HOLDING HANDS

When making separate hands that are going to be holding some object, it is easiest if you first cut out the top profile of the hand, drill a hole large enough for the object to fit through, then saw out the side profile of the hand.

6. LEGS

On the patterns where the legs are together, rather than spread apart, you may want to separate them slightly by sawing on a line from the bottom of the feet, up to where the crotch would be. You can do this with your bandsaw, or a coping saw. This line will help you keep the legs symmetrical and centered on the body.

7. STARS

An easy way to make stars on "patriotic" Santas is to take a stylus or toothpick and put a dot of White paint where you want the star to be. Starting inside the dot, while the paint is still wet, drag the tip of the stylus or toothpick toward the edge and out to make a line. Do this for all five points of the star. The bigger you make the dot of paint to begin with, and the further you drag each line outside of the dot, the bigger the star will be.

8. POM-POMS

If you don't want to try carving the "pom-pom" ball on Santa's hat, you can make one the easy way by using unpainted wooden beads which can be obtained at most craft stores. Buy various sizes, then use one which best fits the hat after the head and hat are carved. Carve a flat spot on the hat, and glue the bead to it. If the bead has a hole in it, fill the hole with wood filler after the glue dries. This method is the most realistic one I have found for making the pom-poms.

GENERAL PAINTING SUGGESTIONS

I have included some **suggested** colors and paintbrushes for all patterns. If you have a preference for a different color scheme, by all means use it. After all, it's your carving, and you can paint it any way you desire.

I have also listed the colors produced by DecoArt and their identification numbers, which I have found to be suitable for painting these carvings. I have used these colors, and the results were excellent. I hope this will help minimize your confusion when trying to sort through the maze of paint brands and colors at your hobby or craft store.

The best paintbrushes I have found, for the money, are made by the Royal Brush Mfg. Company. They come in a wide assortment of sizes and shapes, are durable, and, most importantly, are affordable. In general, here are the ones I use and recommend for painting your carvings.

Royal Golden Taklon series 250 Round, size 0 and 00: Details such as eyes and other small areas.
Royal Golden Taklon series 170 Cat's Tongue, size 2 and 4: Large areas.
Royal Golden Taklon series 150 Short Shader, size 2 and 4: Blending colors. (For example, when blending a "blush" color into the flesh color on faces, hands, etc.)

You may have heard and read this a million times, but when painting your carvings, keep the word **THIN** in mind. What you want to do is stain the wood to give it some color and life, but you don't want the paint so thick that it covers up the beauty of the wood. **NOTE:** When painting faces and hair, I generally use a little thicker mixture of paint than I use on the rest of the carving. I want the face to be a bit more intense than the rest of the carving, since the head and face is what sets most of the mood for the carving.

Suggested Colors
General Colors
Titanium White #DA1 (Eyes, highlights in eyes, beards and hair)
Buttermilk #DA3 (Fur on coat)
French Vanilla #DA184 (Fur on coat)
Sand #DA4 (Fur on coat)
Lamp Black #DA67 (Eye dots, boots, mittens, belts)
Burnt Sienna #DA63 (Boots, belts)
Fleshtone #DA78 (Face, hands, other skin areas)
Blush Flesh #DA110 ('Blushing' on cheeks and lips to give a "windburned" effect)
Baby Blue #DA42 (Eye dots)
Camel #DA191 (Bags)
Sable Brown #DA61 (Bags)
Cadmium Yellow #DA10 (To blend with Red in lanterns to give a "candle" effect)
Venetian Gold #DA72 (Belt buckles, metal on lanterns.)

Coat/Robe colors:
Santa Red #DA170
Lavender #DA34
True Blue #DA36
Napthol Red #DA104
Plum #DA175
Olive Green #DA56
Holly Green #DA48
Olde Gold #DA176
Calico Red #DA20
Reindeer Moss Green #DA187

"Antiquing:"

Oak Antiquing Gel #DS30 (Use to give some 'age' to the finished carving)

Clear Satin Varnish #DS15 (Use to seal the carving after the antiquing has been done)

If you cannot find these colors locally, you can contact DecoArt at: http: //www.decoart.com. They will be glad to tell you where a dealer is located close to you, and in many cases will provide you with samples of some of the colors for you to try.

Remember: These are only a few of the many colors you can use for your carvings. Should you have other color preferences, use them. Don't be afraid to get wild and experiment with all sorts of color combinations. For those of you (like me), who have difficulty trying to decide which colors work well together, most hobby and art supply stores sell inexpensive color wheels which will show you colors that work together, and colors that oppose each other. I have listed a few combinations here, for illustrative purposes:

MAIN COLOR	CONTRAST COLOR
Red	Green
Orange	Blue
Yellow	Violet

A good color wheel will not only show you main and contrast colors, it will also show colors that blend.

"ANTIQUING" the PROJECT

Once the paint is dry, you may want to "age" your carving with an antiquing product in order to help tone down the colors a bit. I have had excellent results using antiquing gels made by DecoArt. These are available at hobby and craft stores. They come in various colors, so you can create different effects.

Brush a coat of antiquing gel on the wood, then wipe it off using a damp rag or sponge. It is your option how much you wipe off. After the antiquing is dry, I like to finish my carvings with a coat of brush-on acrylic varnish. DecoArt also makes an excellent varnish. I prefer the one that leaves a Satin finish. This particular finish is not too flat or too glossy, but leaves a "soft" look to the completed carving. (*I usually put a coat of varnish on the face, hands and other flesh areas BEFORE I antique the carving*). This will prevent these areas from absorbing too much antiquing color.

Patterns

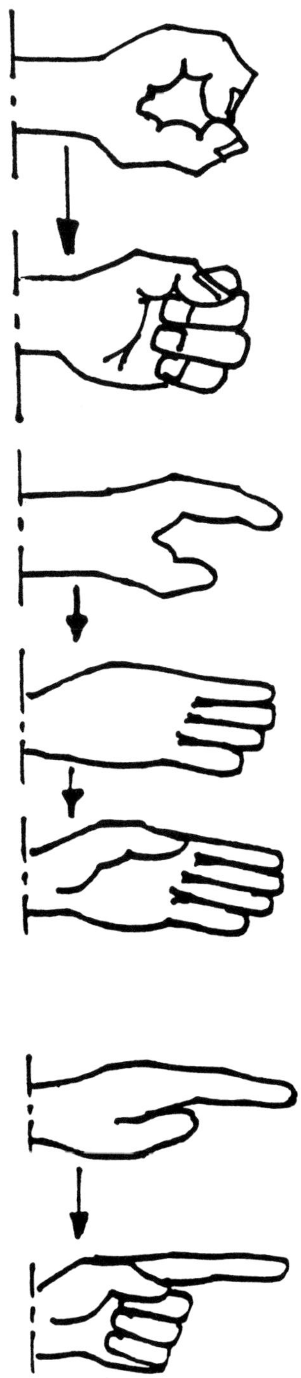

HAND STUDIES

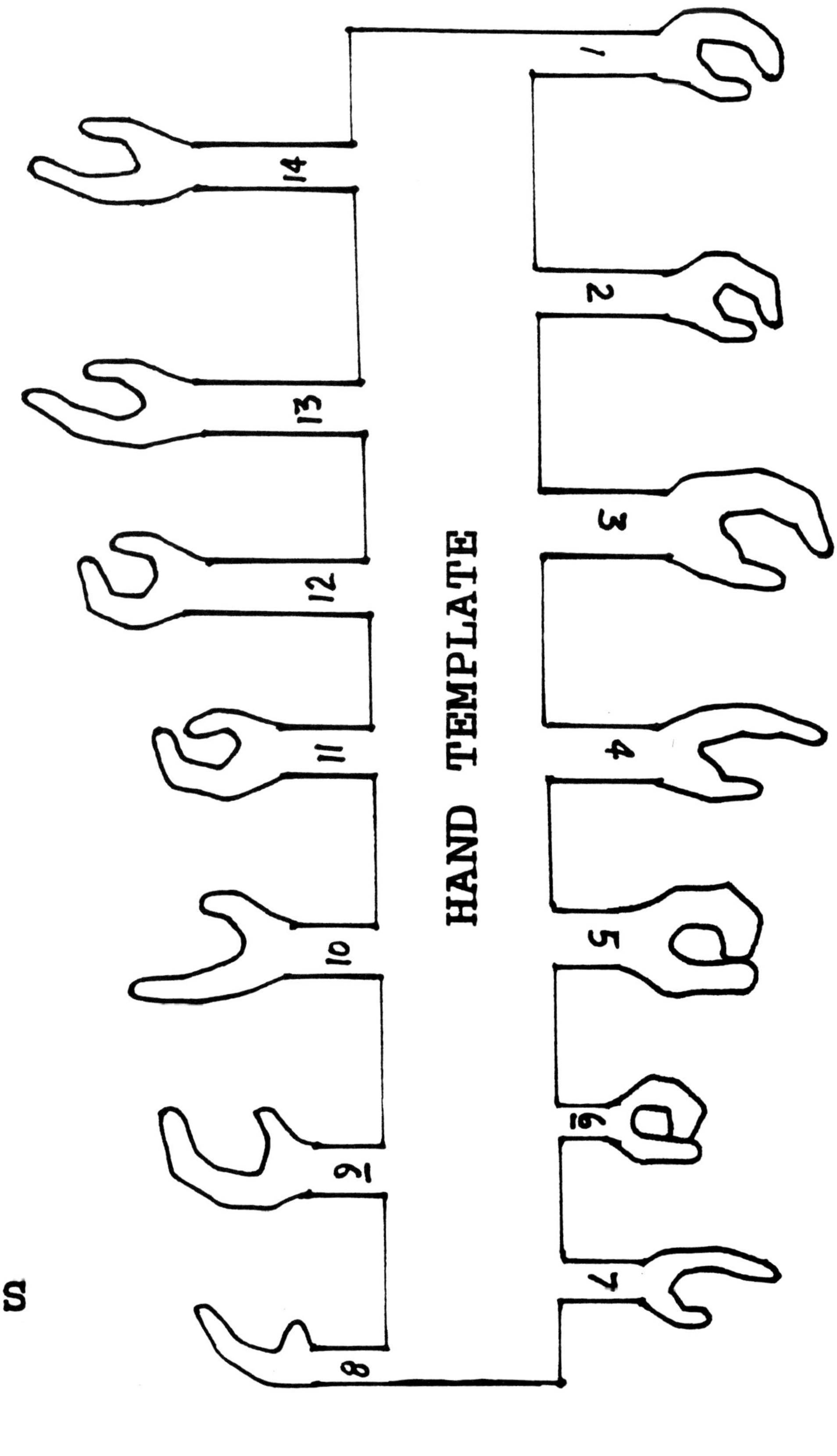

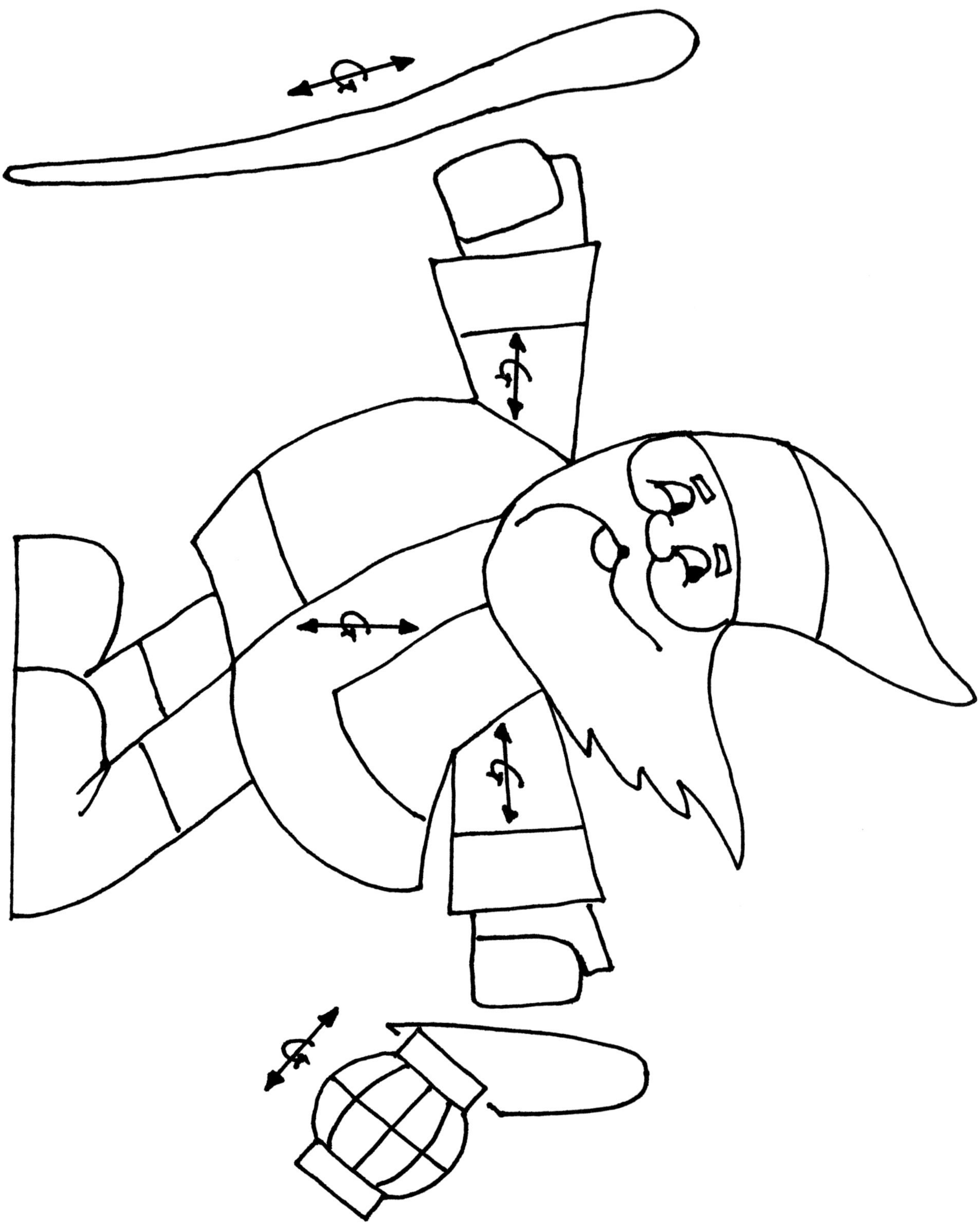

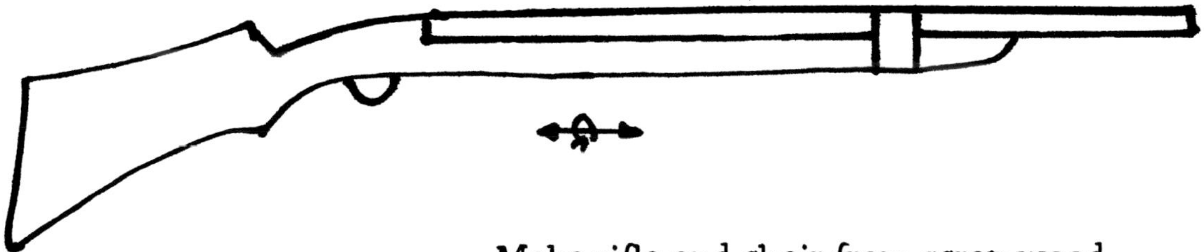

Make rifle and chair from scrap wood.

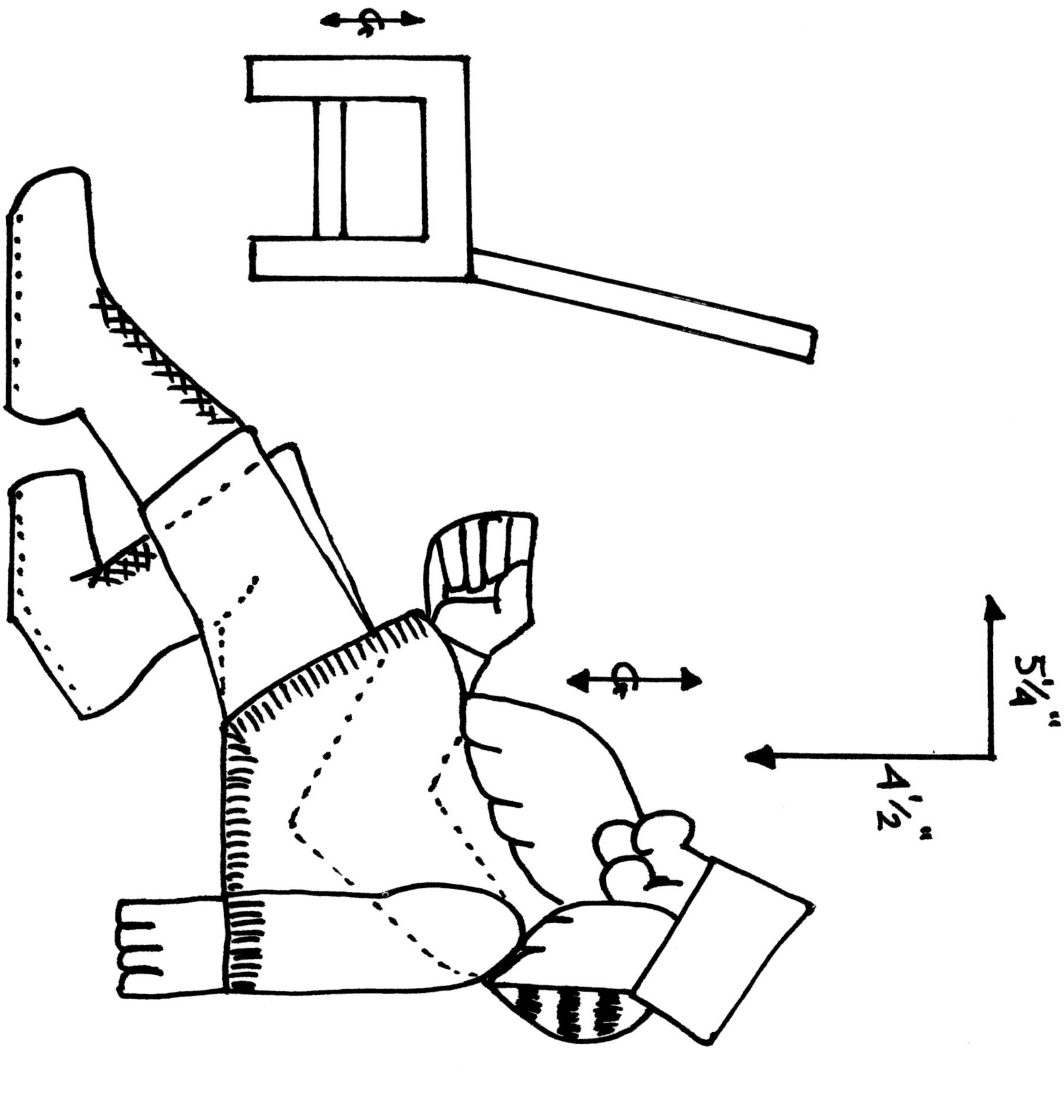

Drill hole thru hand to hold the rifle. Christmas ornaments are made from small wooden beads. Hang them from rifle barrel using sewing thread.

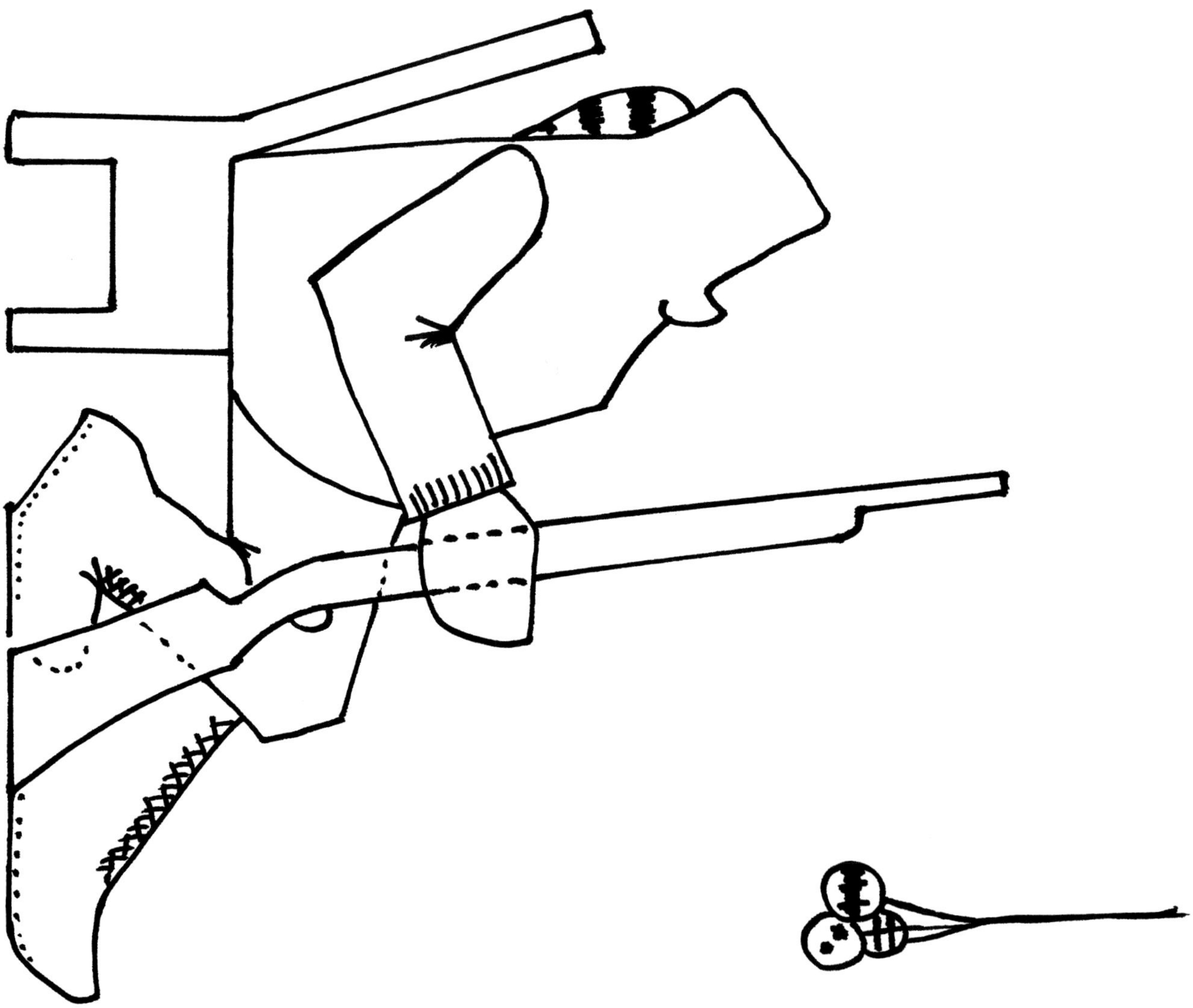

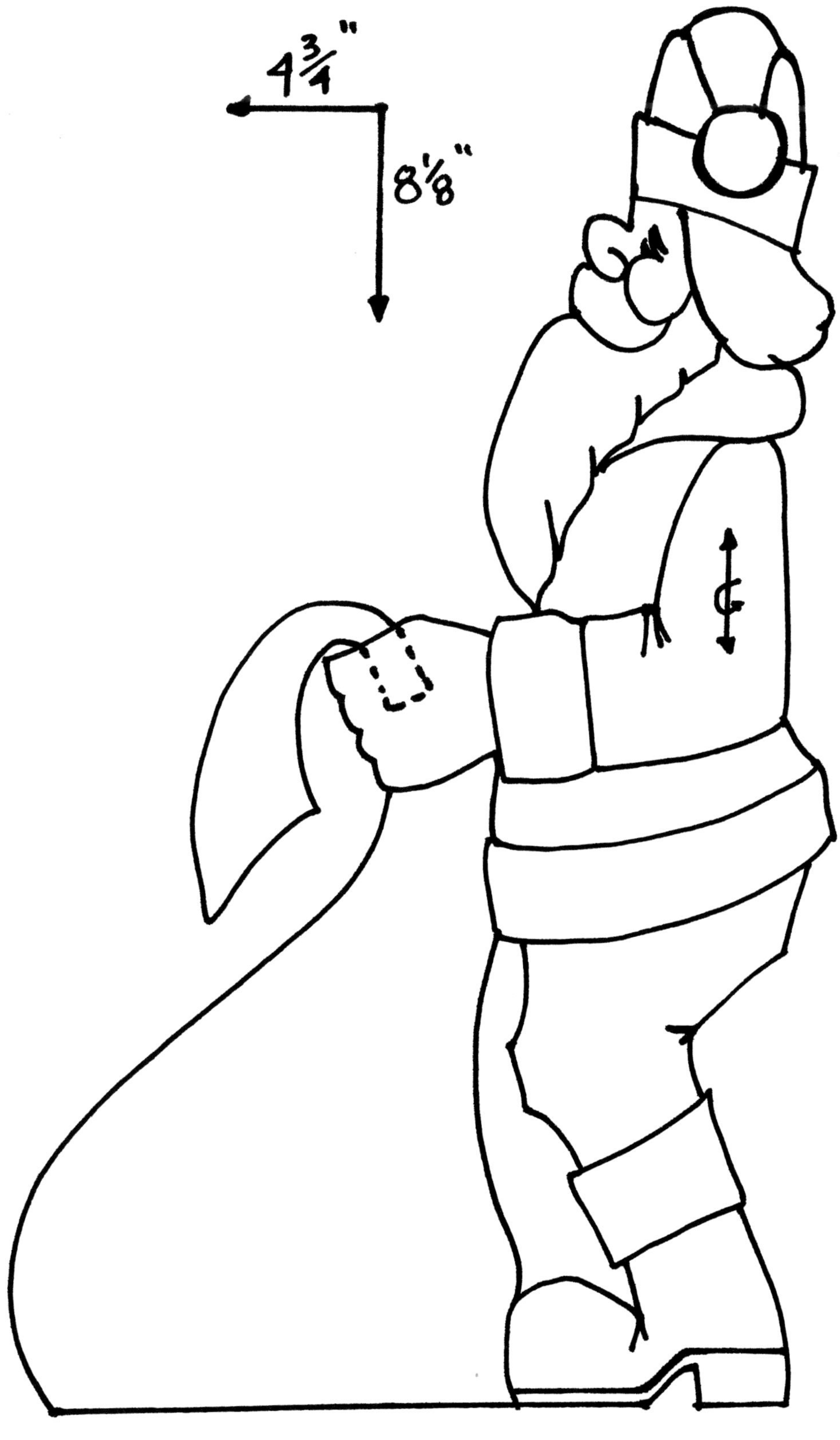
4 3/4"
8 1/8"

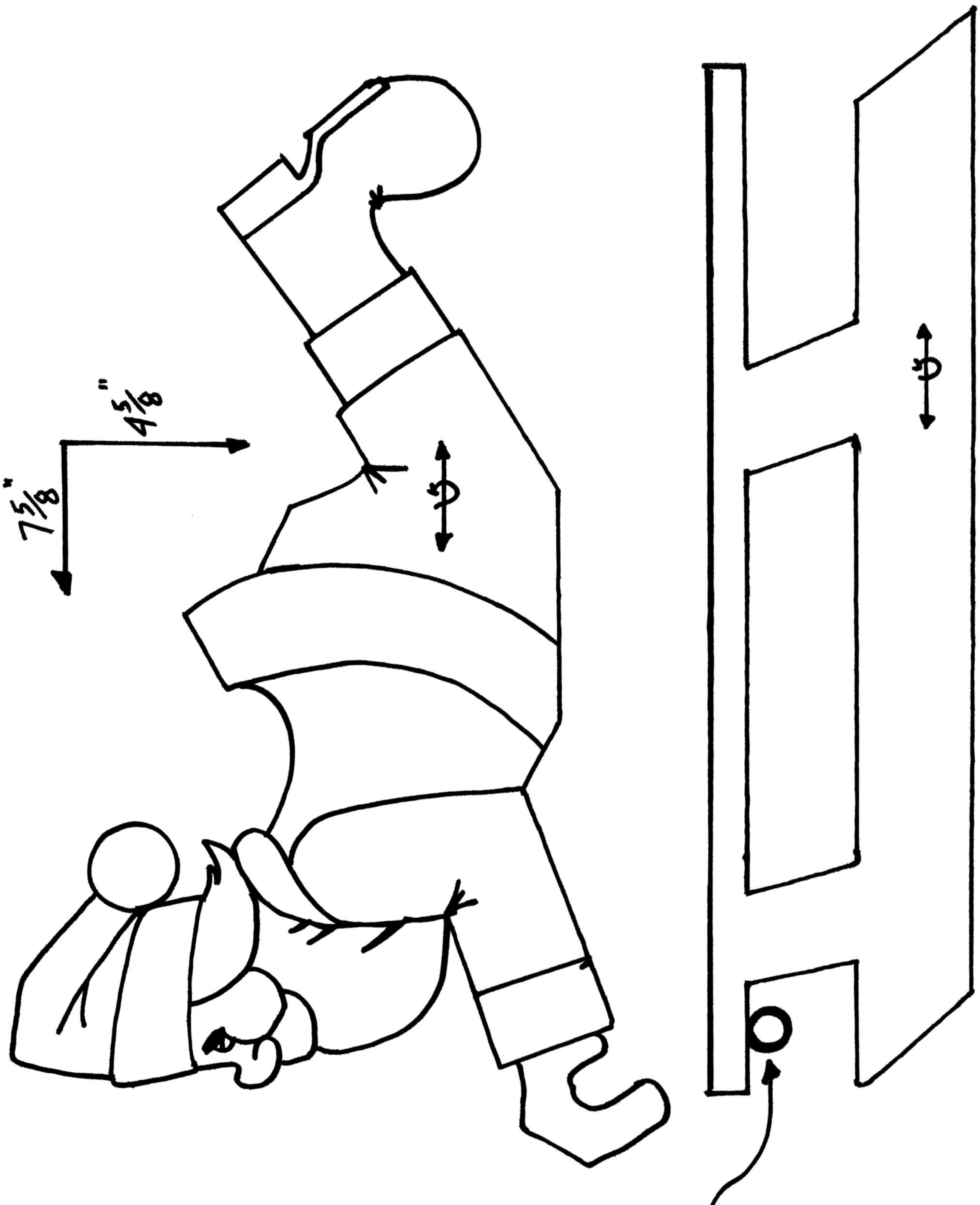

Sled is made from scrap wood. Steering bar is made from a wooden dowel. Hands should grasp the bar when the Santa is placed flat on top of the sled.

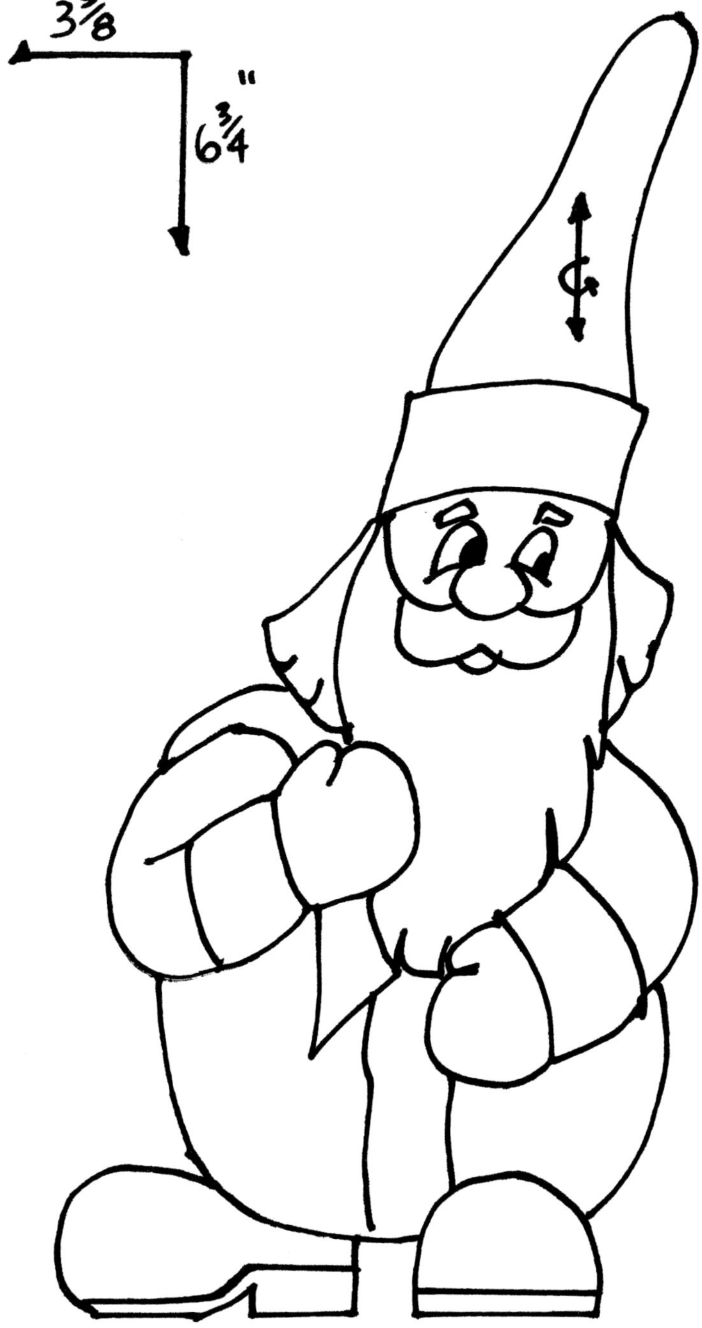
3 3/8"
6 3/4"

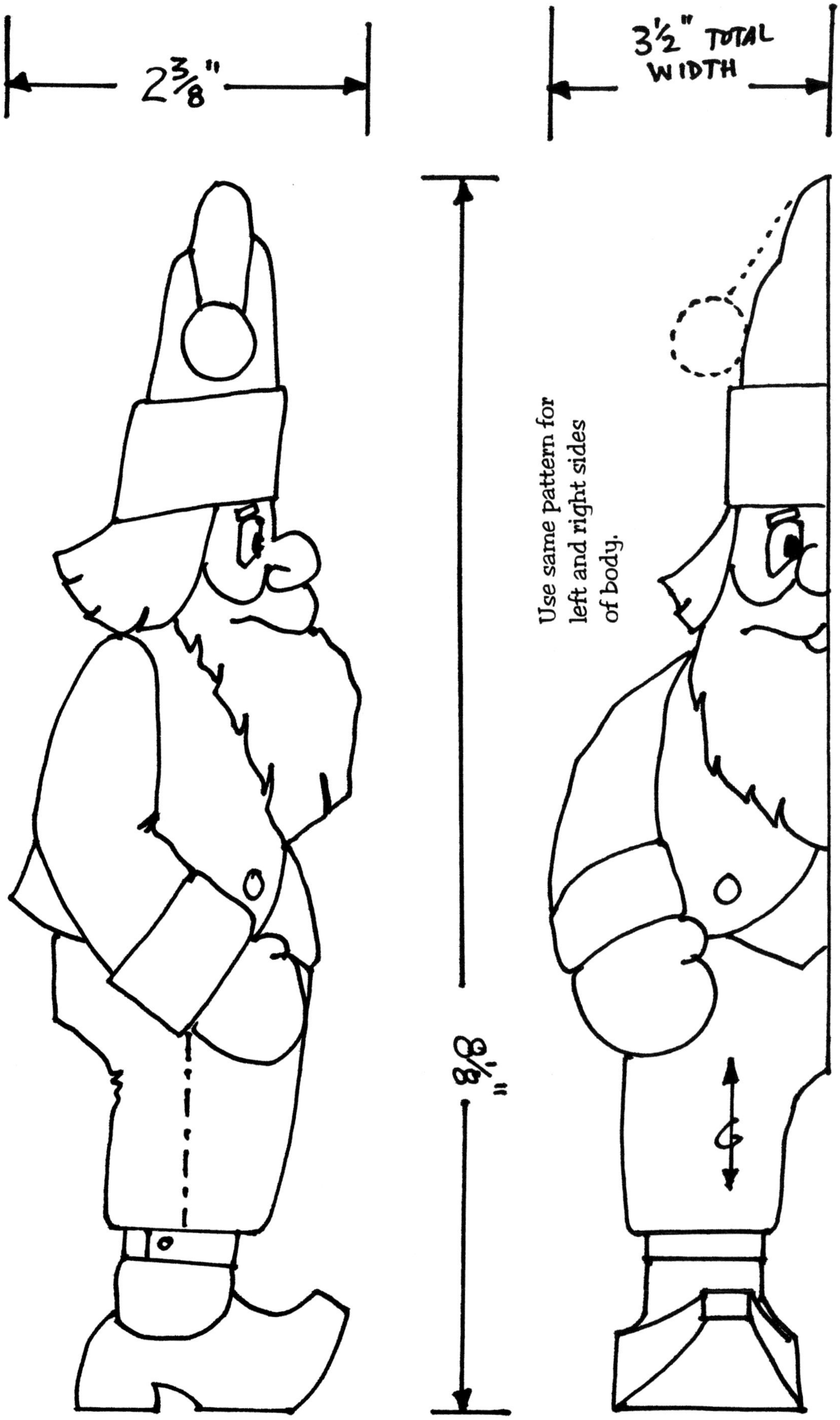
2 3/8"
3 1/2" TOTAL WIDTH
8 1/8"
Use same pattern for left and right sides of body.

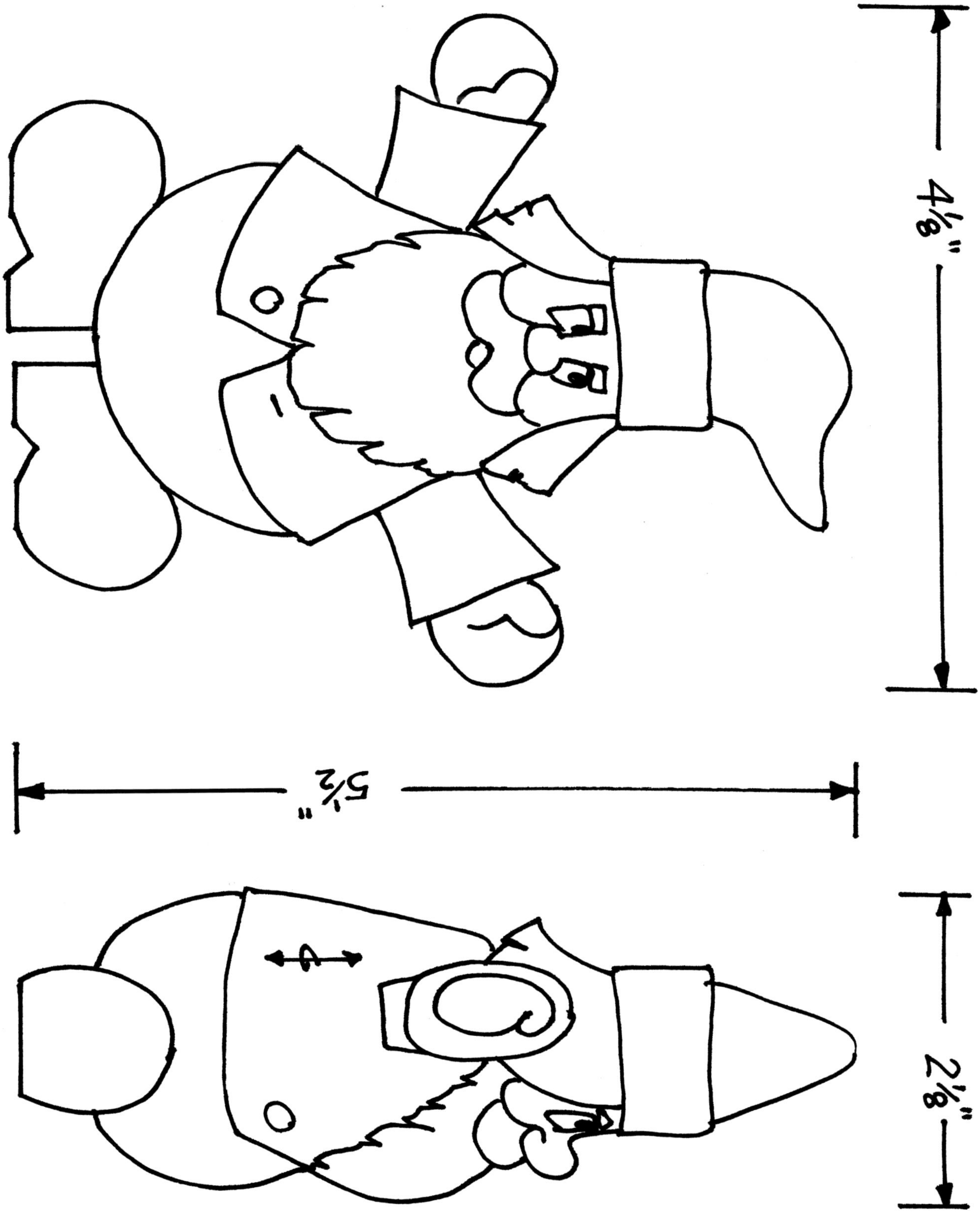
4⅛"
5½"
2⅞"

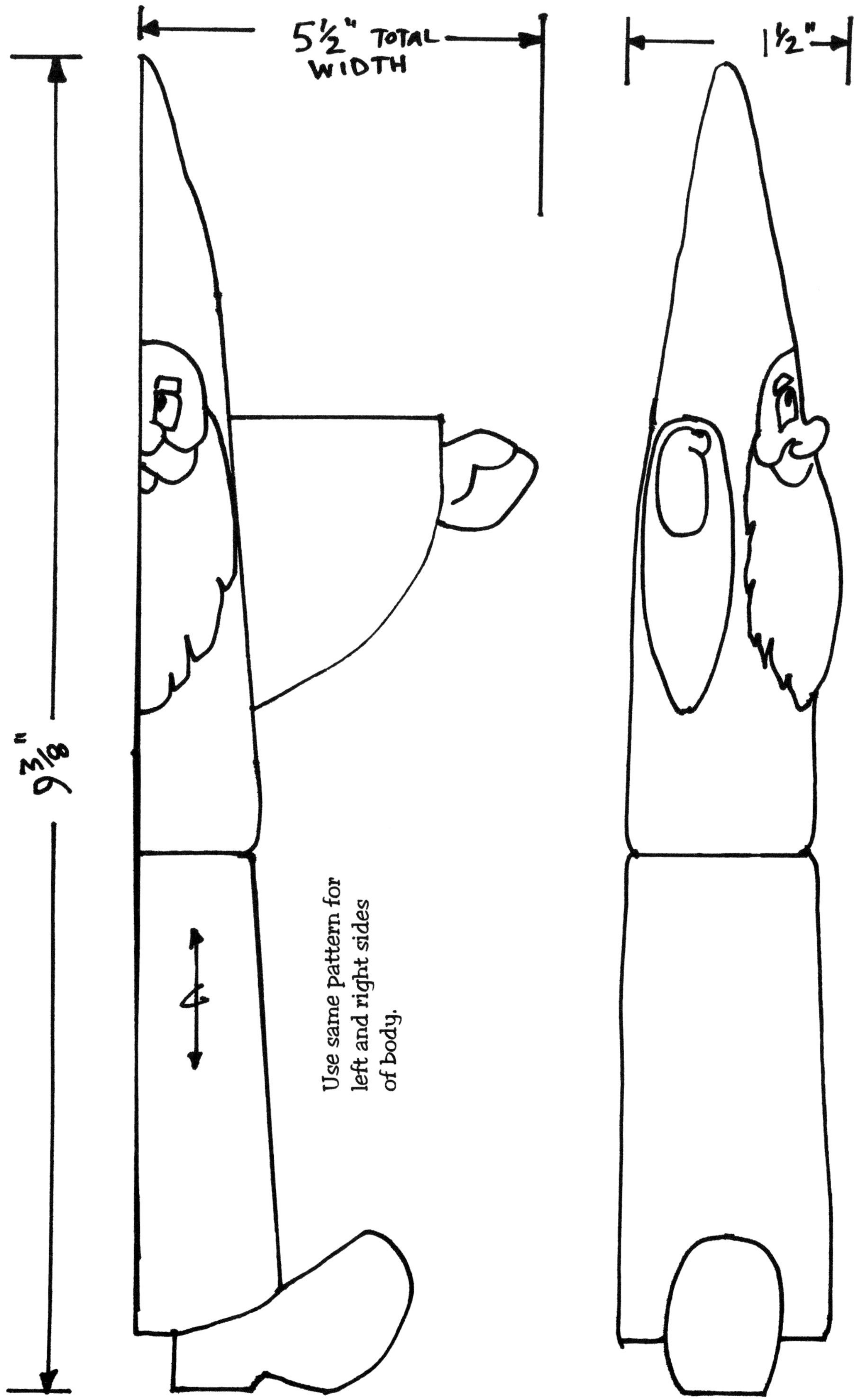
5½" TOTAL WIDTH
1½"
9 3/8"
Use same pattern for left and right sides of body.

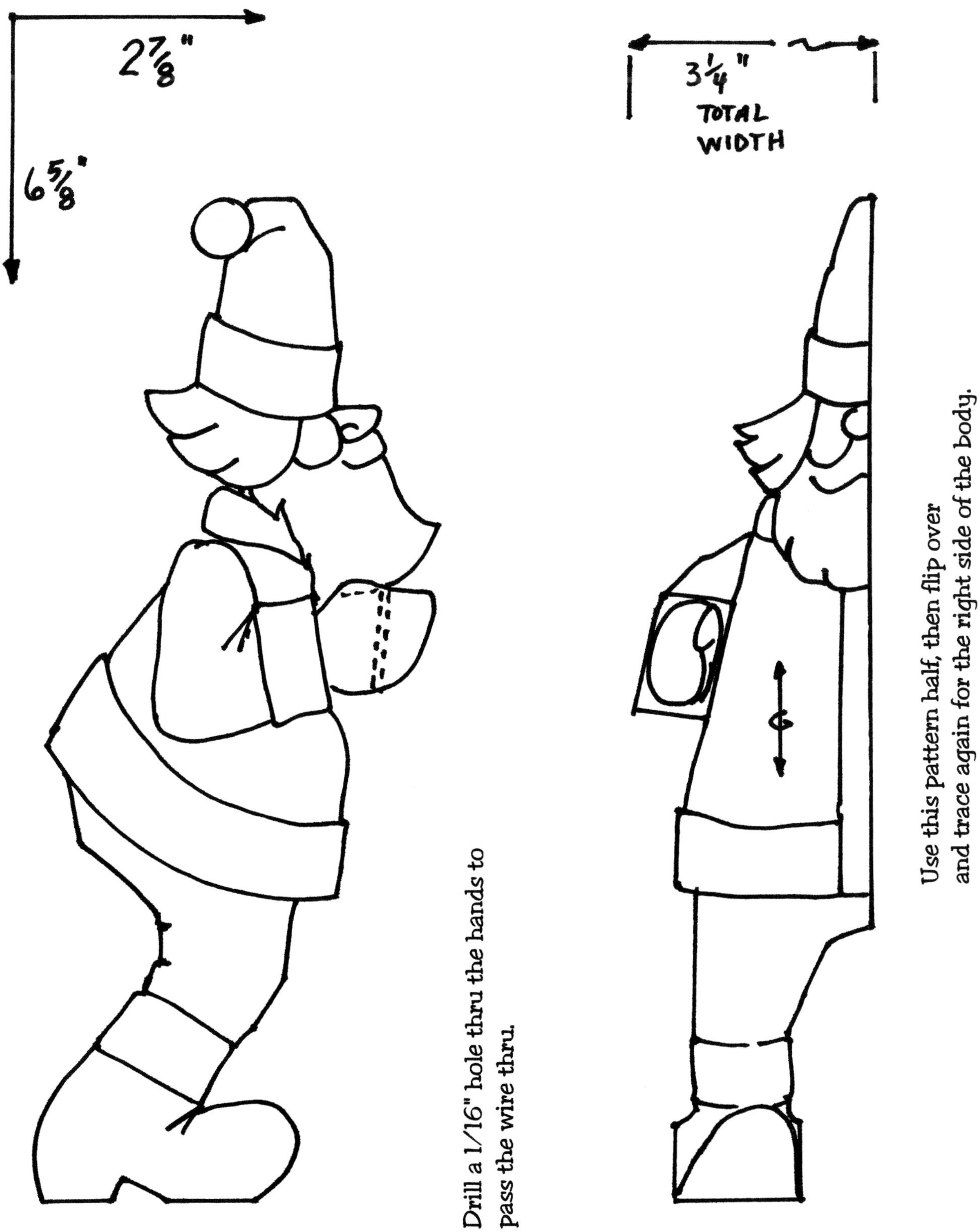
2 7/8"
6 5/8"
3 1/4"
TOTAL WIDTH
Drill a 1/16" hole thru the hands to pass the wire thru.
Use this pattern half, then flip over and trace again for the right side of the body.

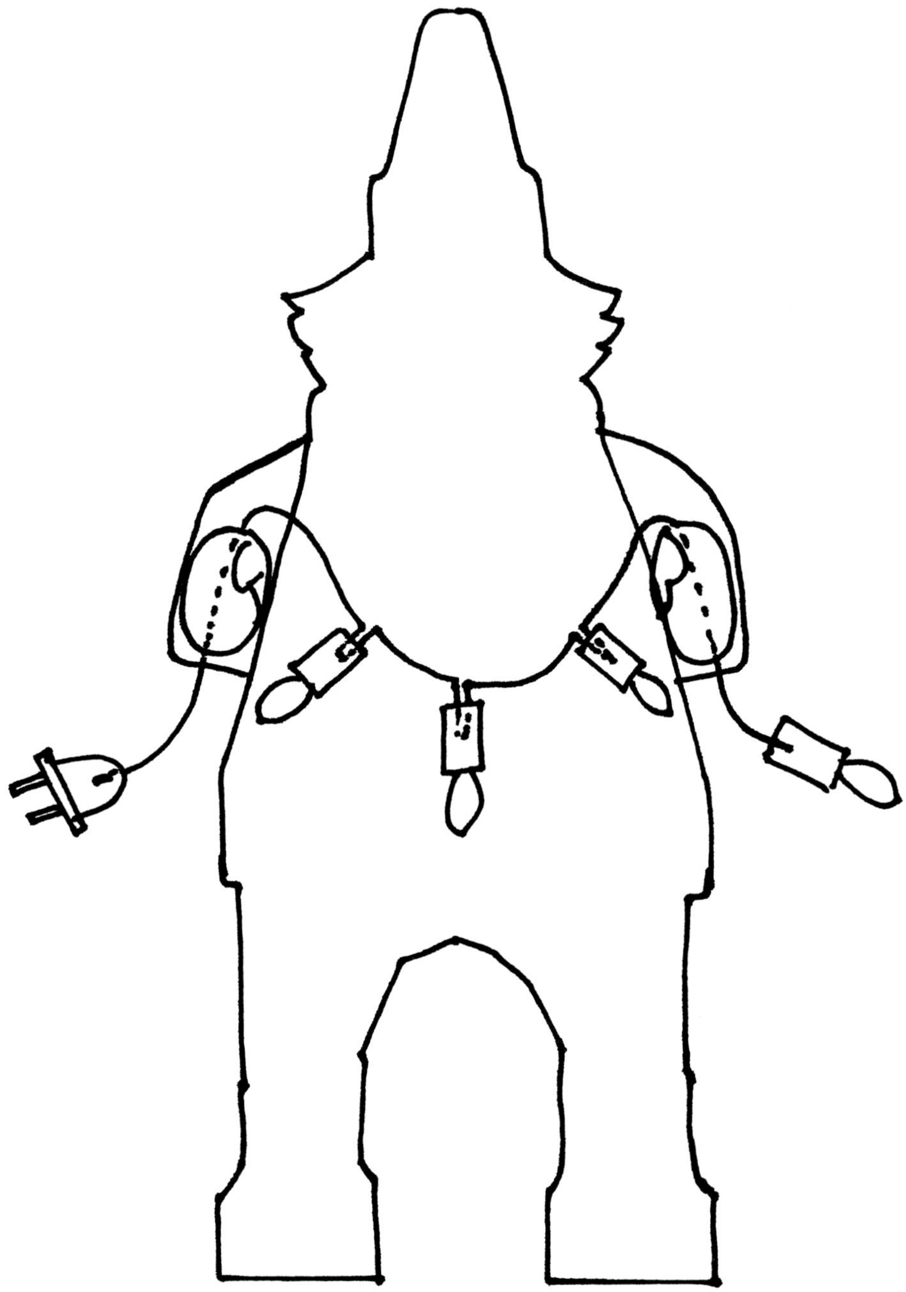

Drill 1/16" holes in plug and lights to accept the wire loops.

Attach carved plug to a loop in one end of wire. Pass thru hand. Put loops in the wire to attach all of the lights, except the last one. Pass wire thru other hand, then attach last light to loop in that end.

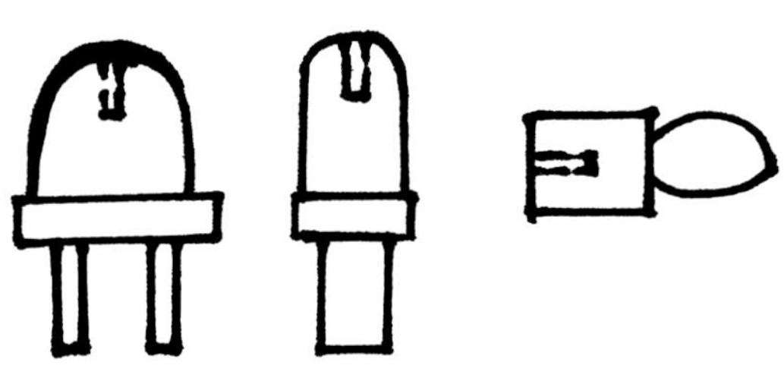

Saw plug and about 8 lights from scrap wood. Carve to shape.

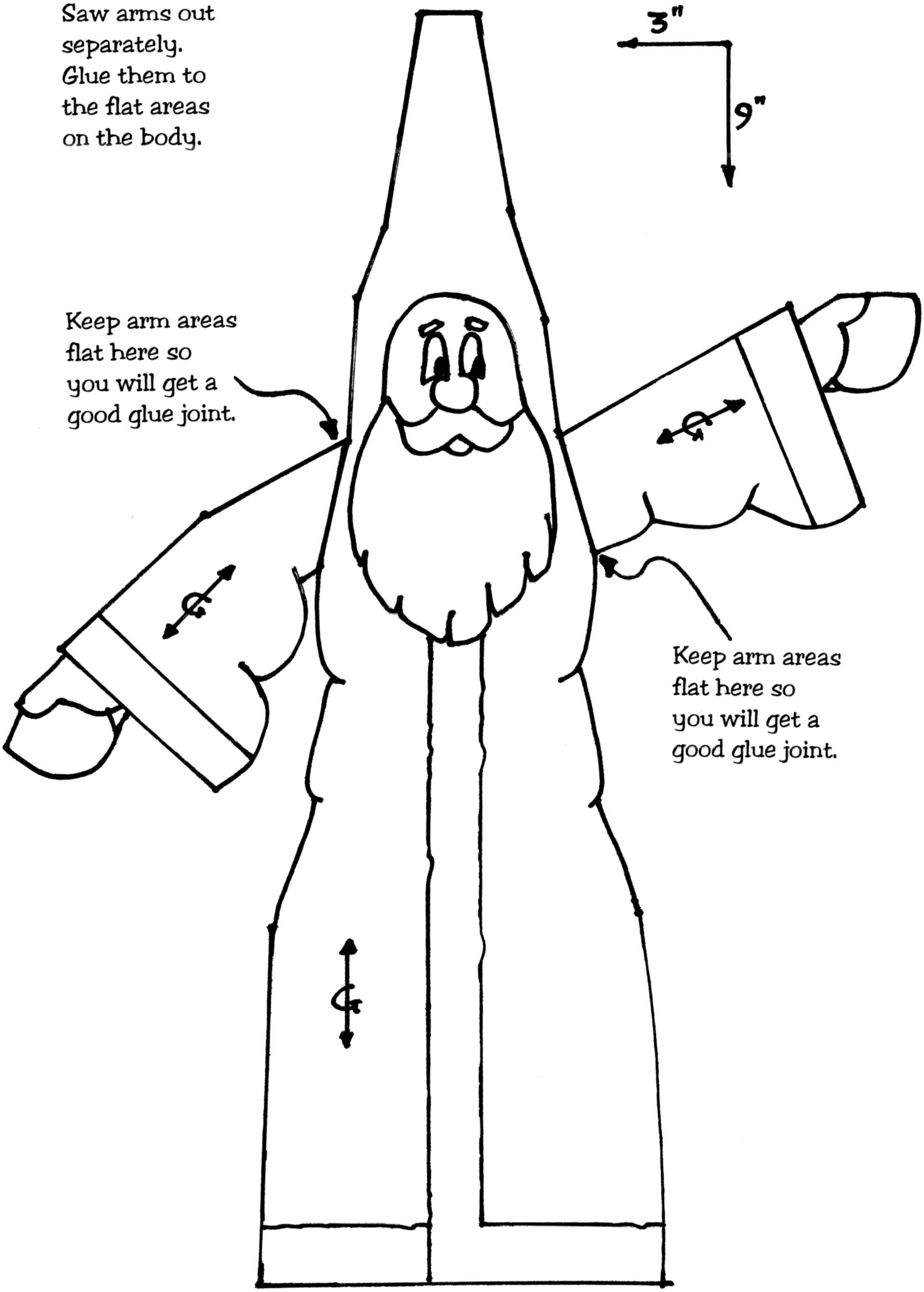
Saw arms out separately. Glue them to the flat areas on the body.
3"
9"
Keep arm areas flat here so you will get a good glue joint.
Keep arm areas flat here so you will get a good glue joint.
G
G
G

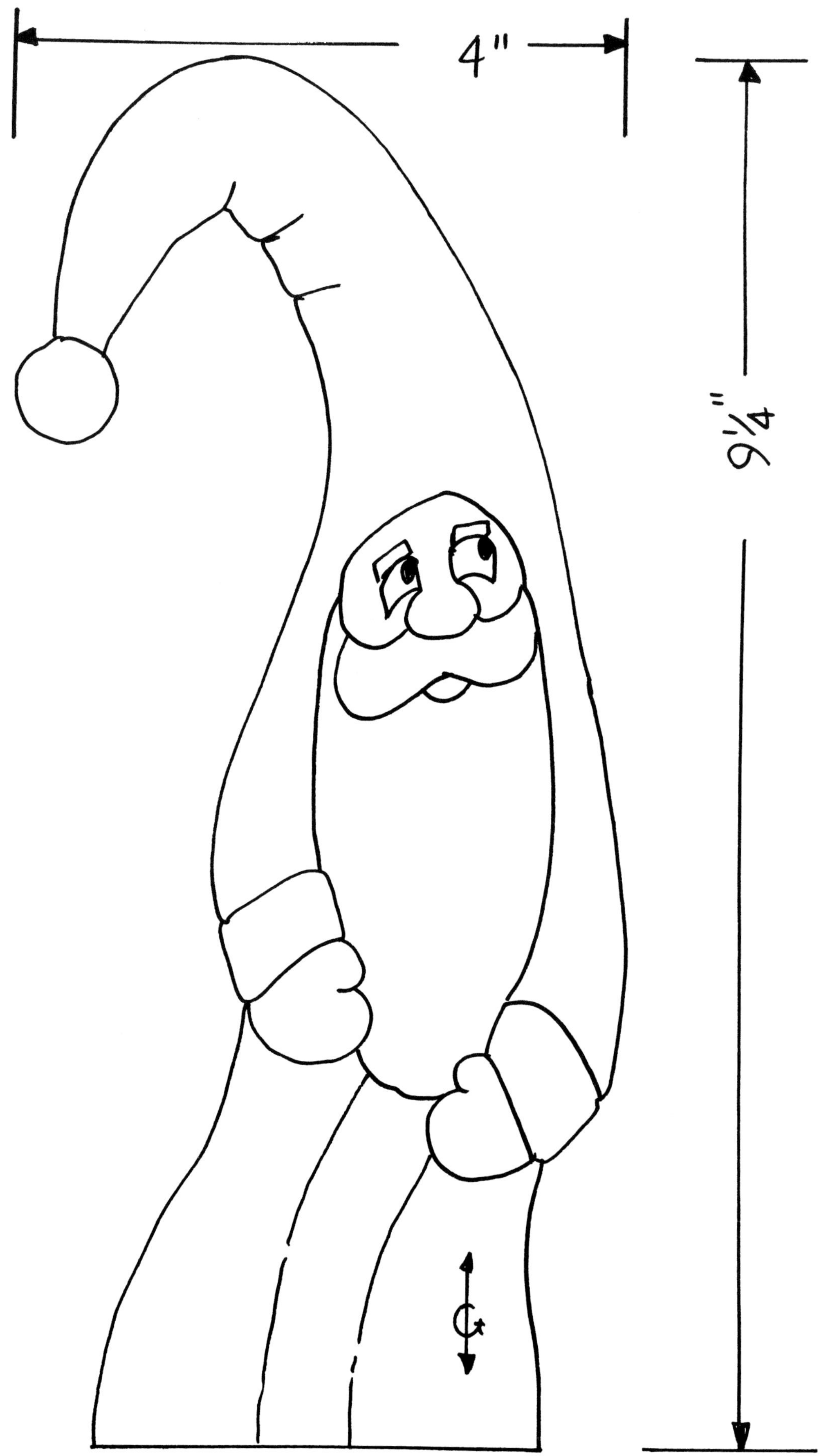
4"
9¼"

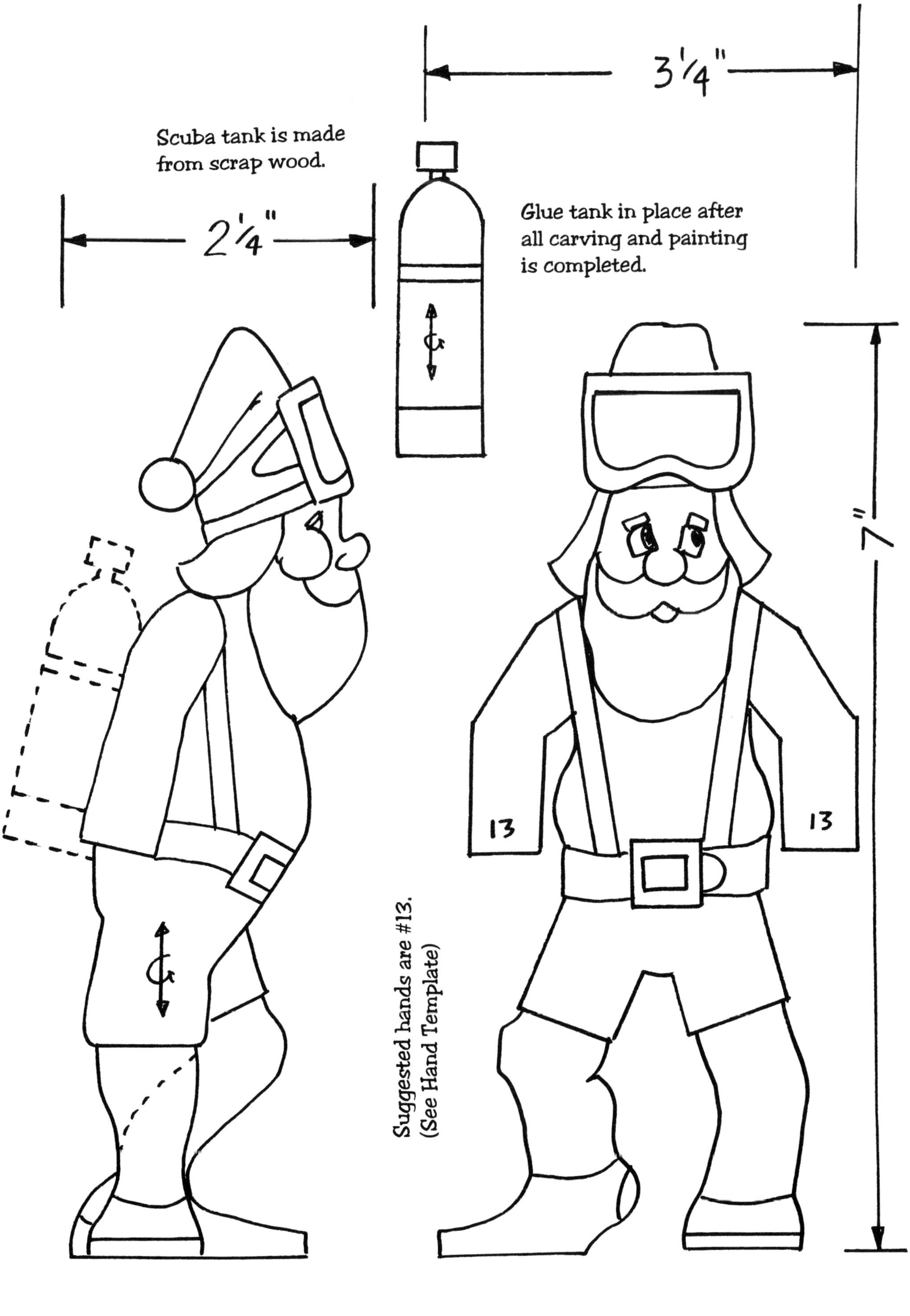

Scuba tank is made from scrap wood.
Glue tank in place after all carving and painting is completed.
2¼"
3¼"
7"
13
13
Suggested hands are #13. (See Hand Template)

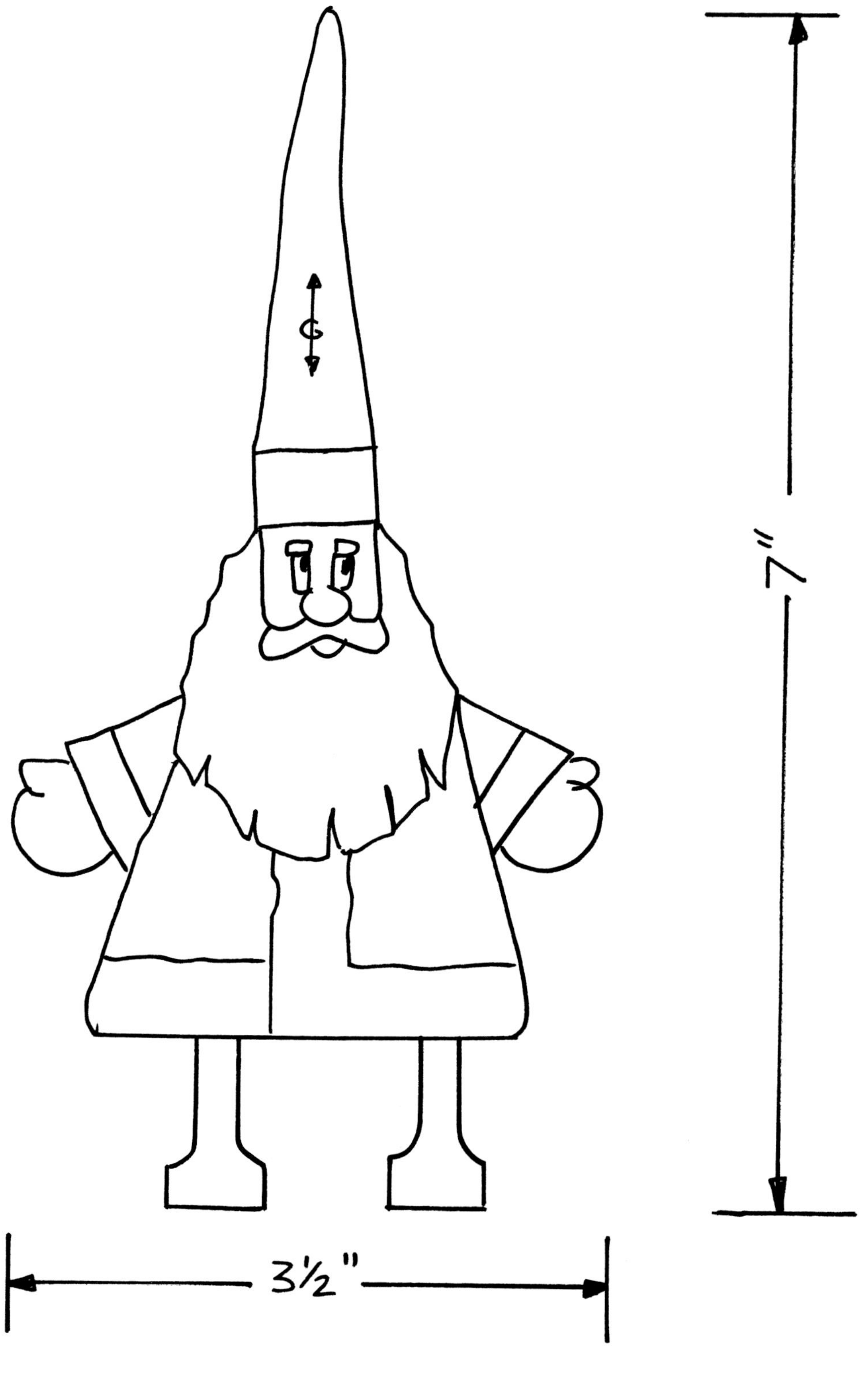
G
7"
3½"

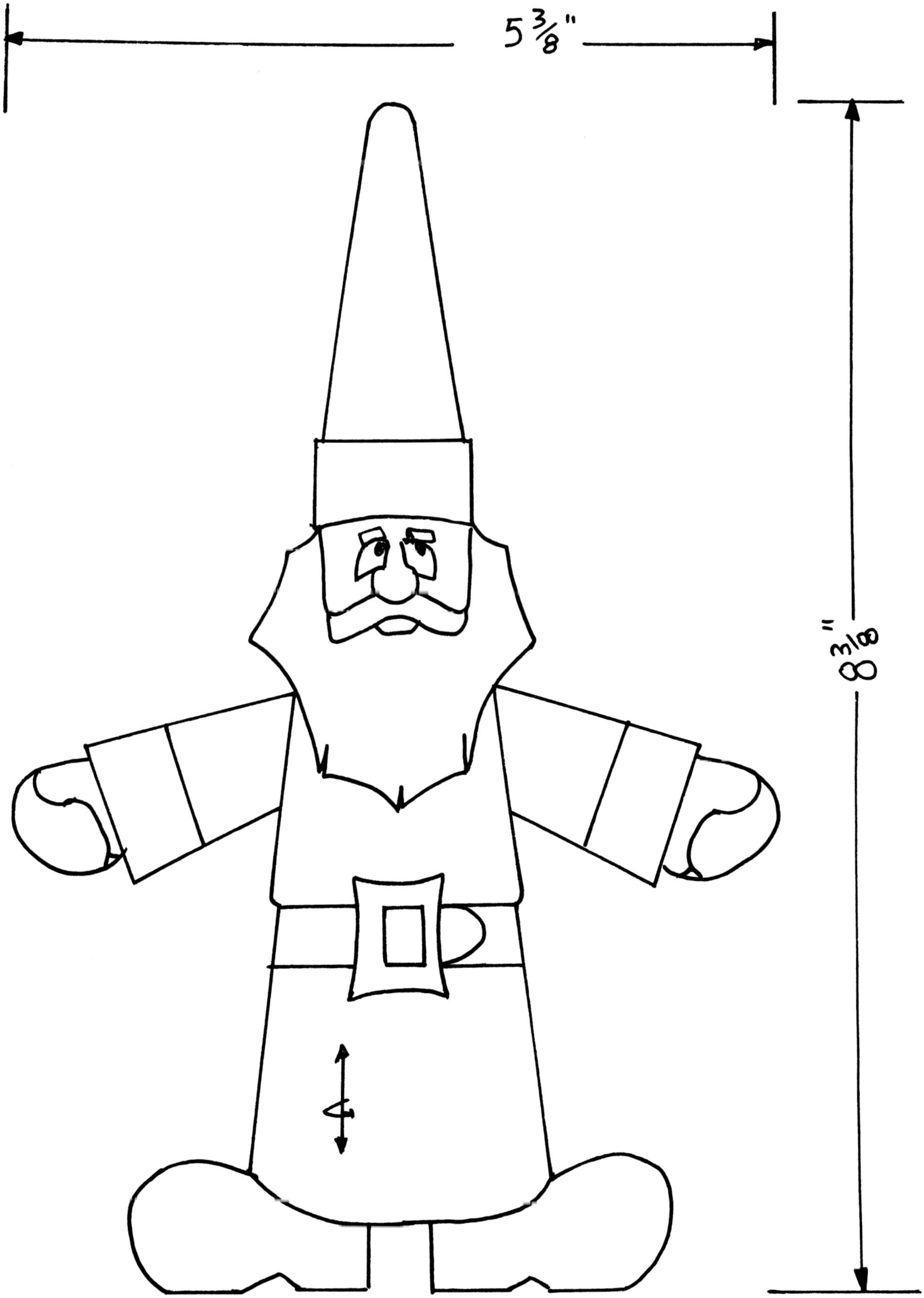
5 3/8"
8 3/8"

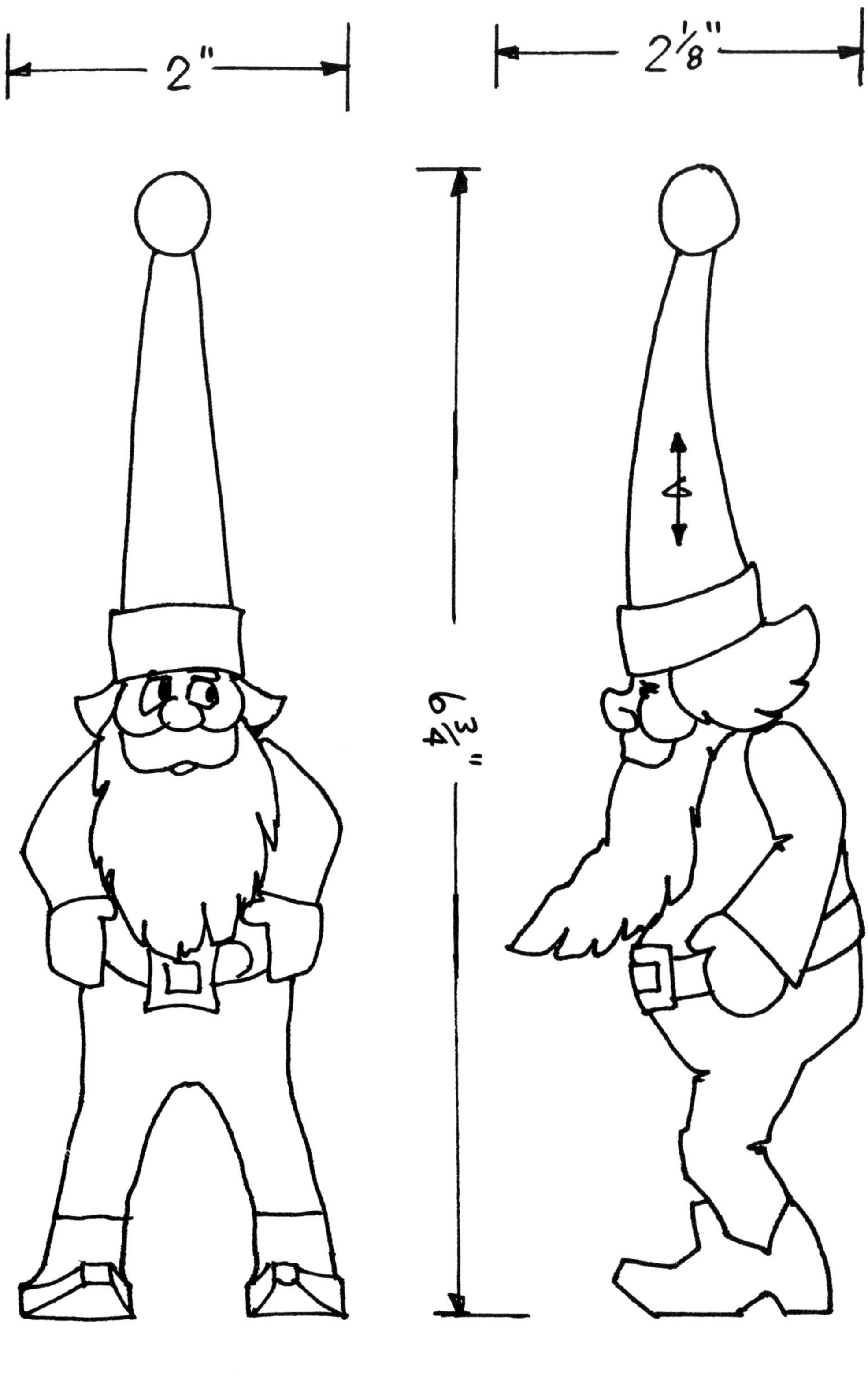

2"
2⅛"
6¾"

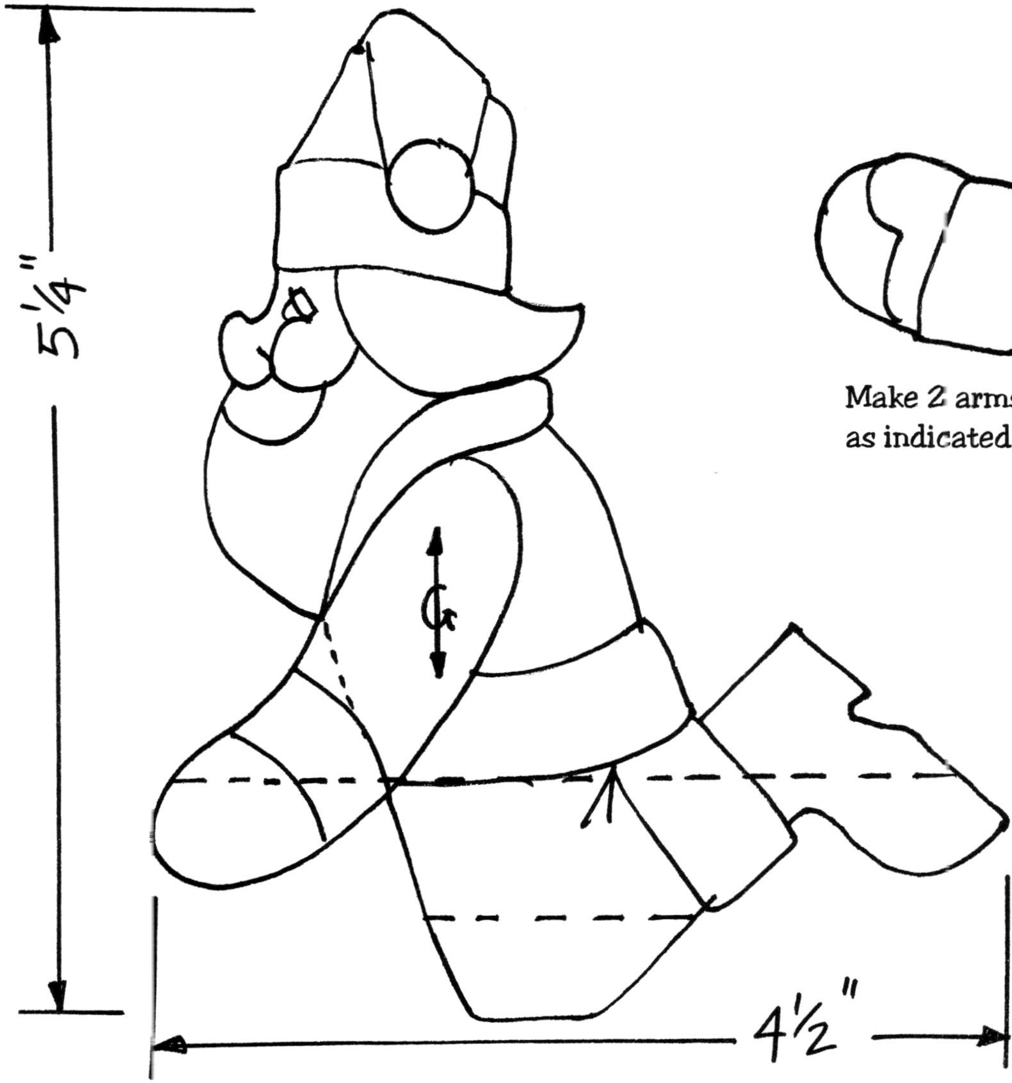

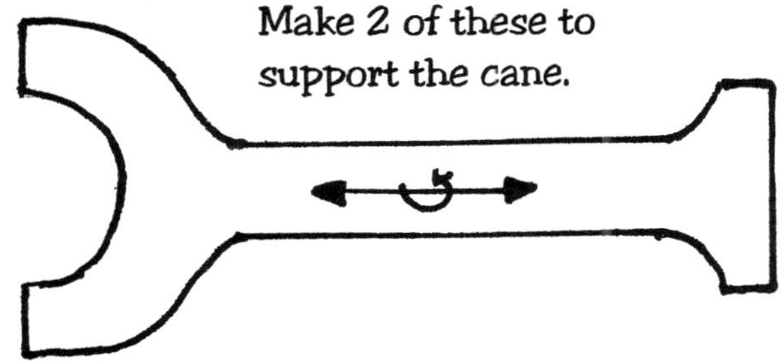

Make 2 of these to support the cane.

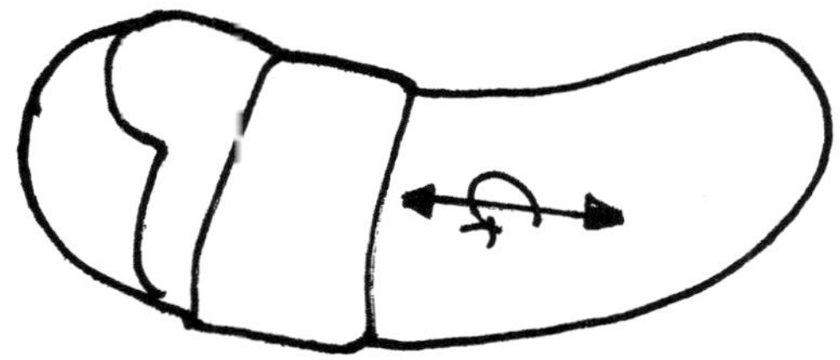

Make 2 arms. Glue in place as indicated on the pattern.

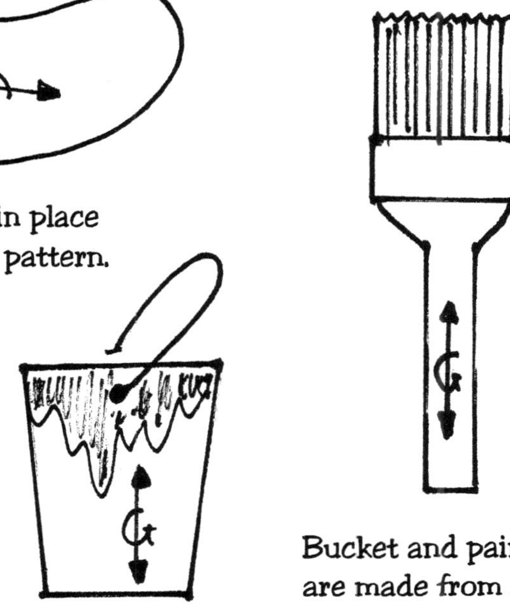

Bucket and paintbrush are made from scrap wood. Use small piece of wire for bucket handle.

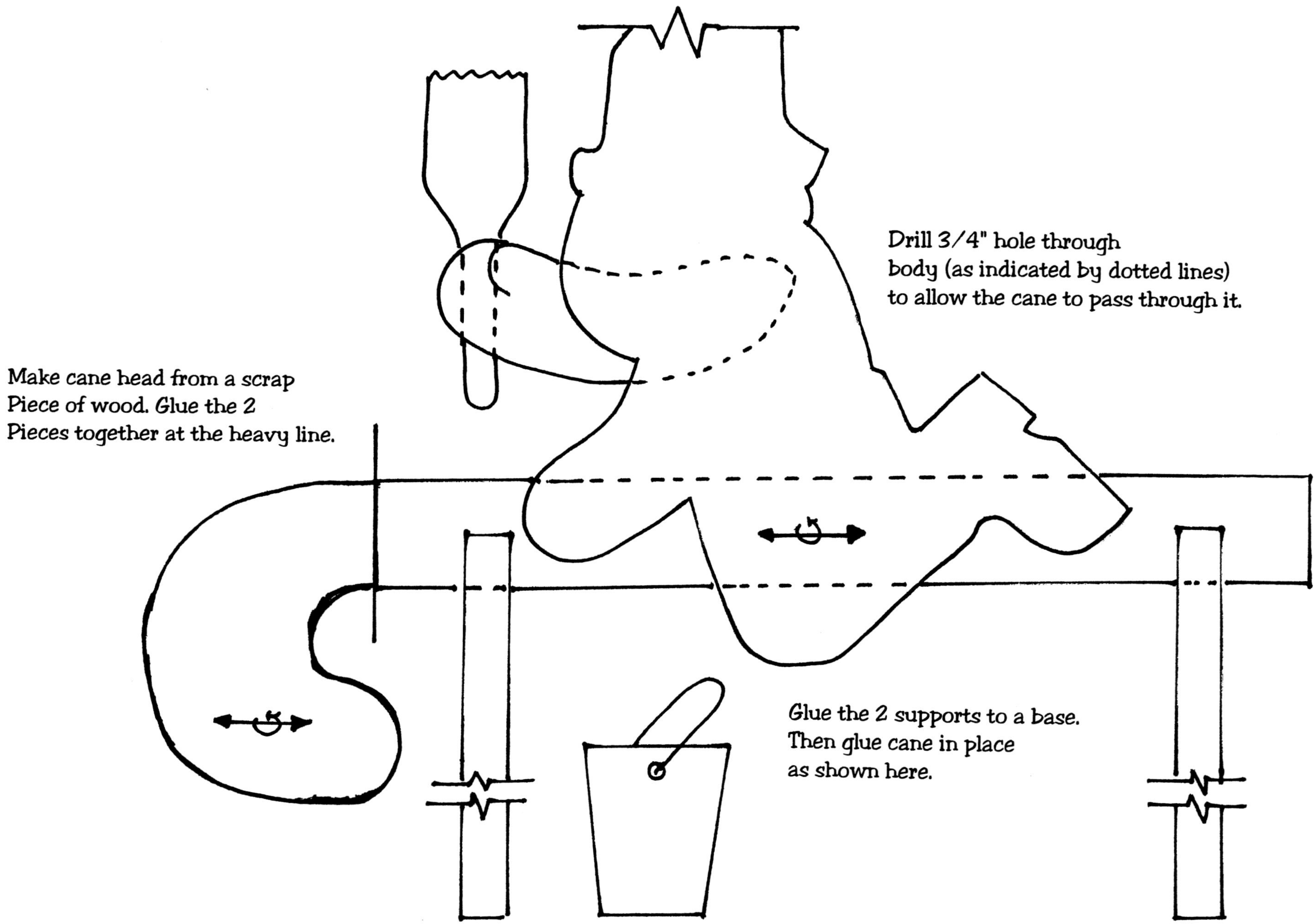
Drill 3/4" hole through
body (as indicated by dotted lines)
to allow the cane to pass through it.
Make cane head from a scrap
Piece of wood. Glue the 2
Pieces together at the heavy line.
Glue the 2 supports to a base.
Then glue cane in place
as shown here.

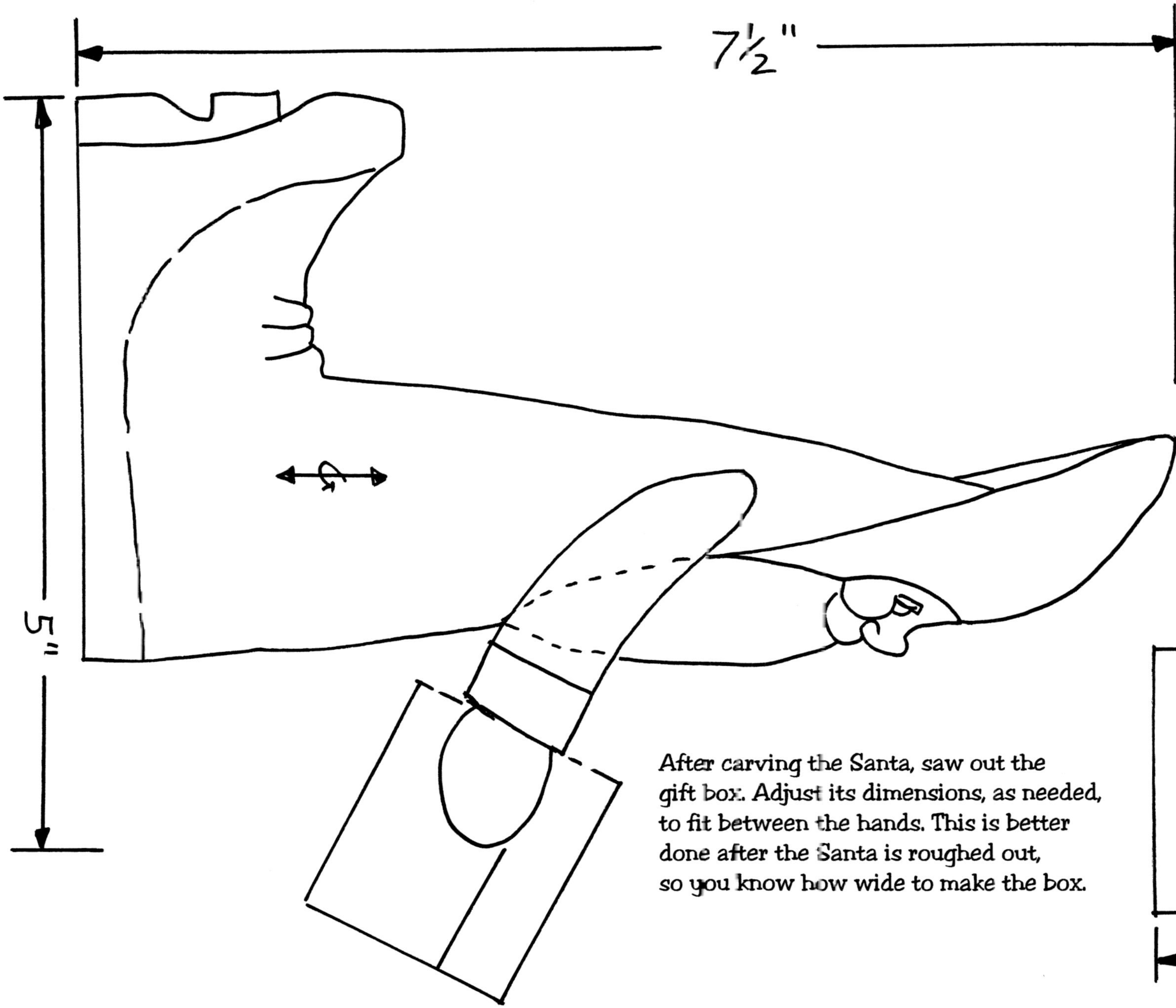

After carving the Santa, saw out the gift box. Adjust its dimensions, as needed, to fit between the hands. This is better done after the Santa is roughed out, so you know how wide to make the box.

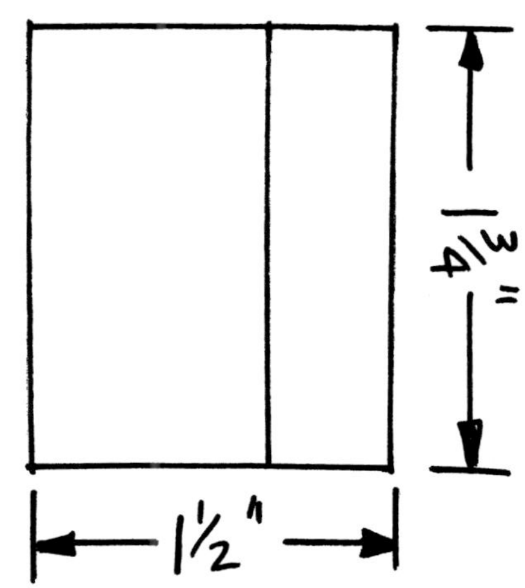

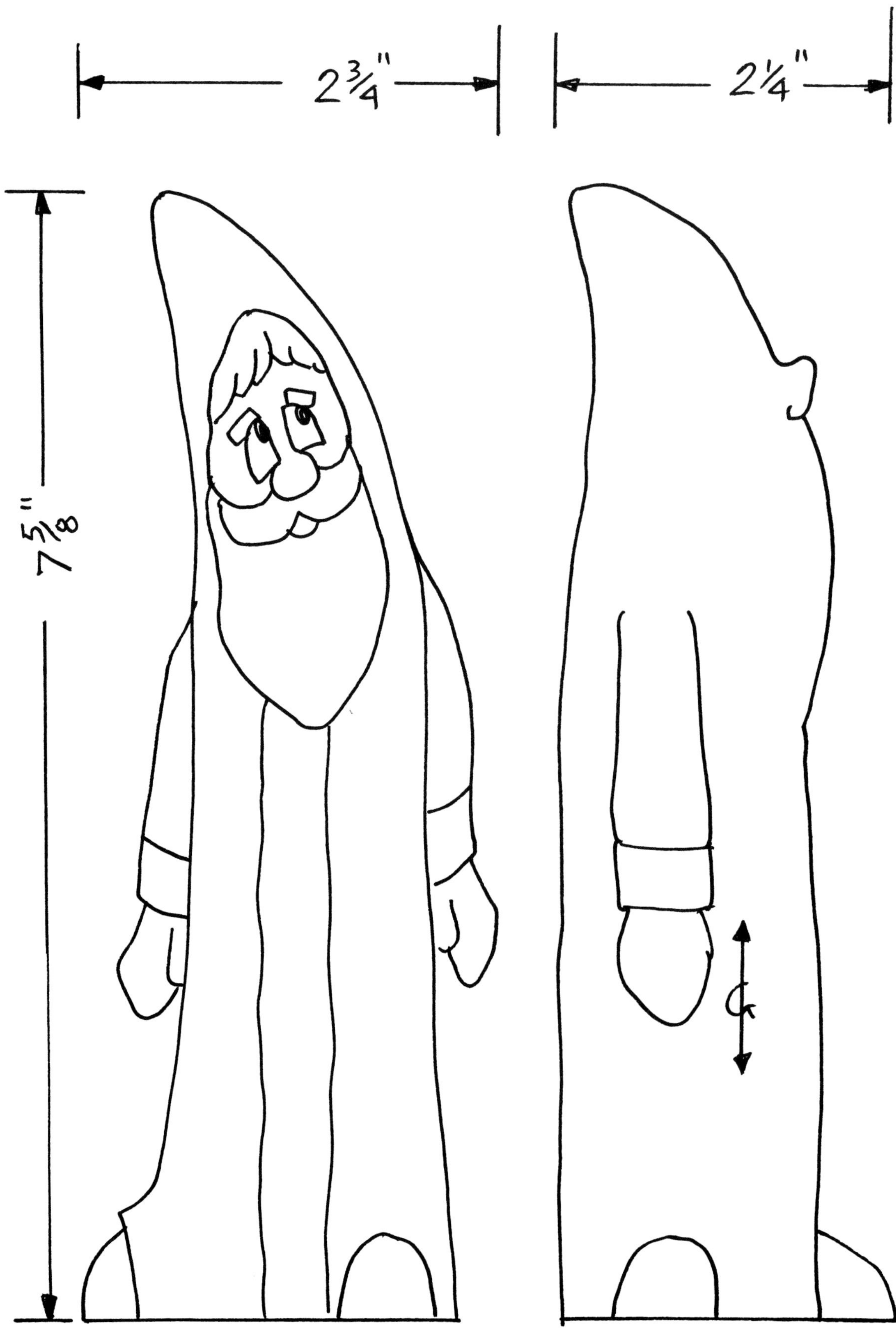
2 3/4"
2 1/4"
7 5/8"

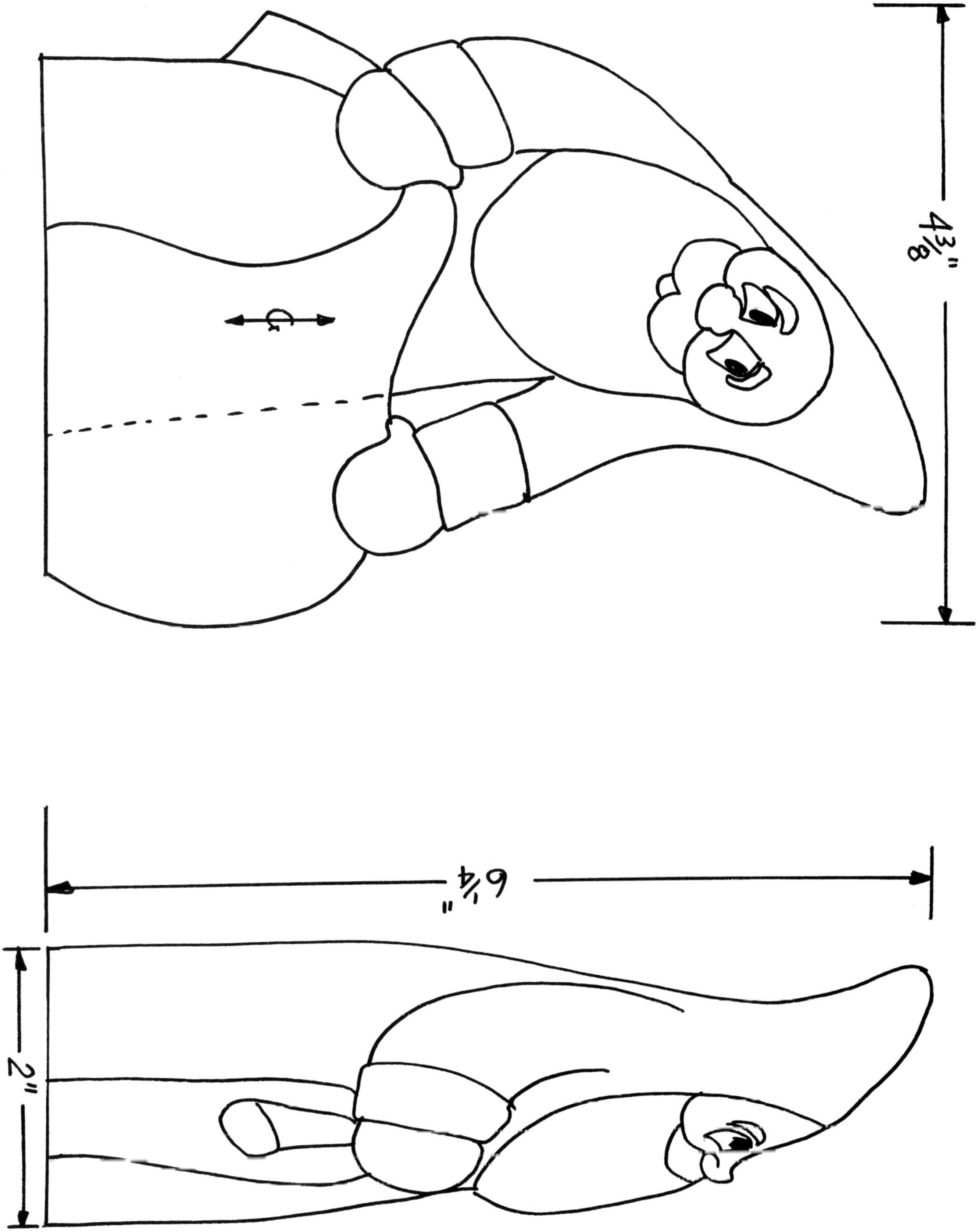
4 3/8"
6 1/4"
2"

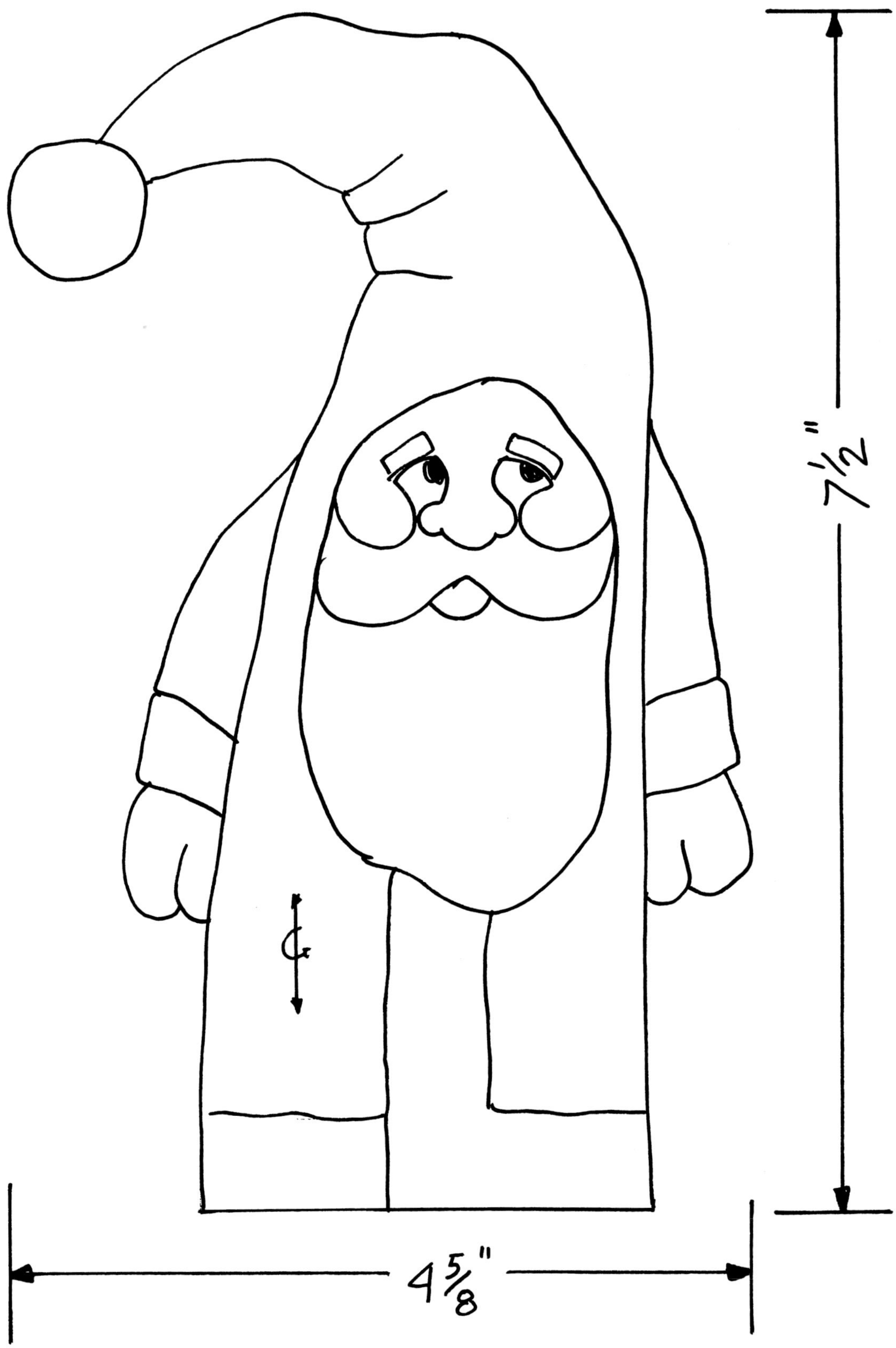
7½"
4⅝"

Carving the Project

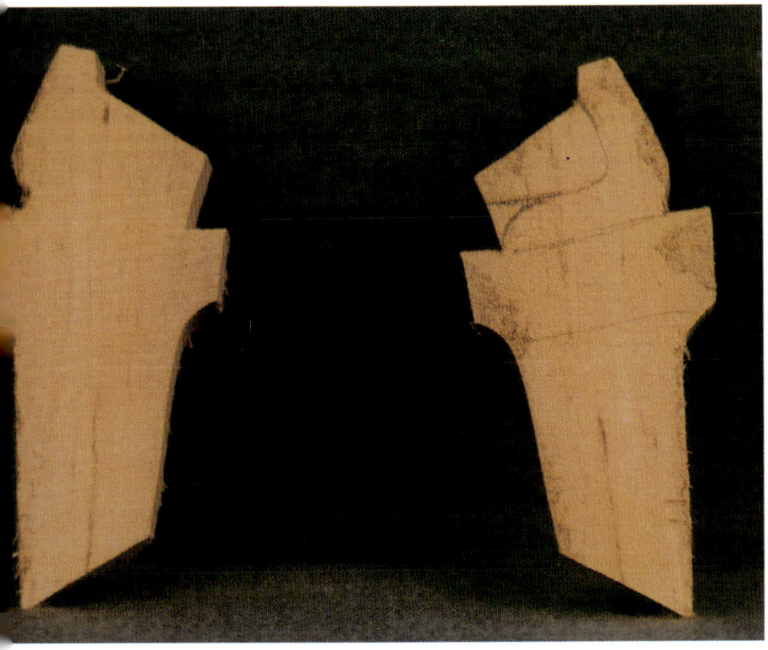

Transfer the arm pattern to a piece of 3/4" thick wood and saw it out. The arms are identical, so saw out two of them. We will carve the right arm step-by-step, then you can use the same steps to carve the other one. Remember to reverse the thumb location when you carve the other arm and hand! Use you own hands as a reference if you get in trouble.

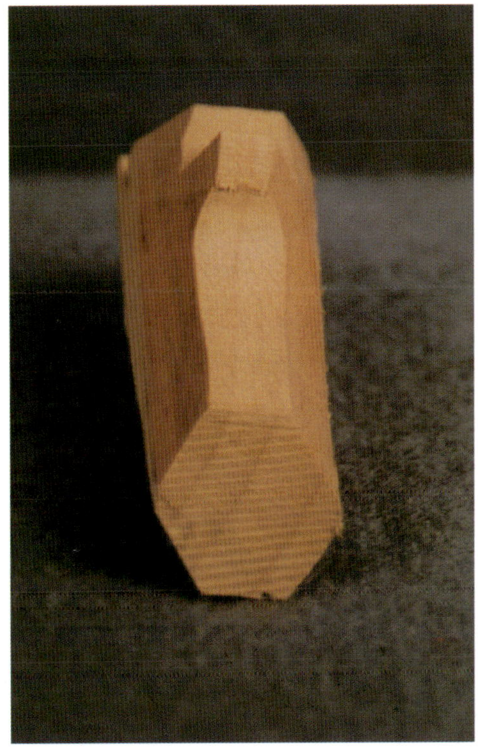

And in this end view.

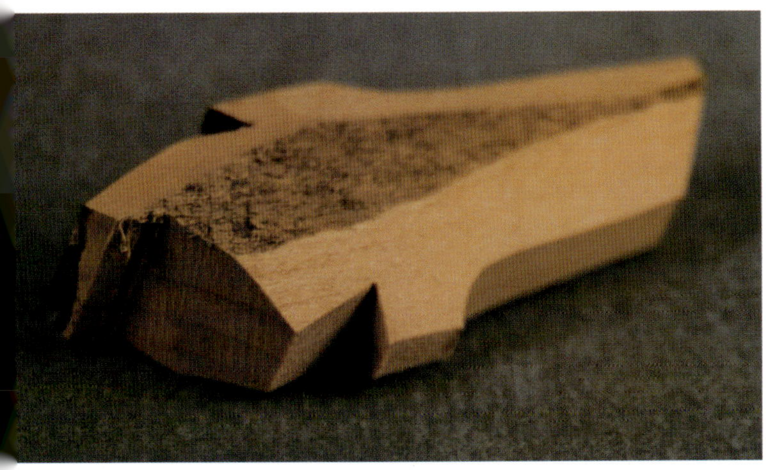

Using your knife, remove all four sharp edges from the arm and hand. This will leave an octagonal-shape, as seen here in this length-wise view...

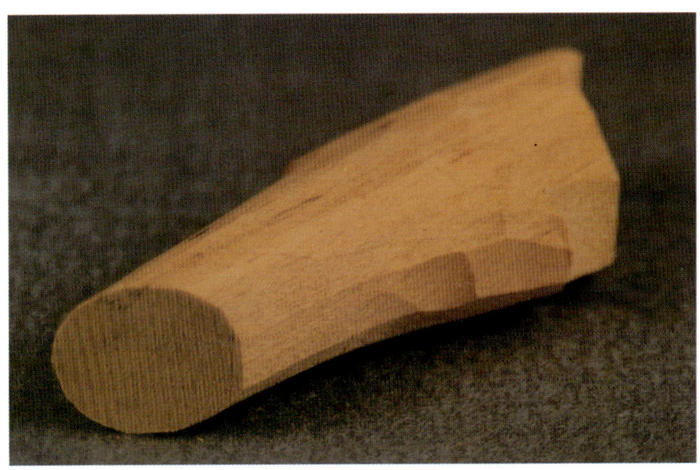

To continue the rounding-off process, continue using your knife to remove the eight sharp edges which the last step created. The arm will now have sixteen small sharp edges, and will be approaching a state of roundness. This is how rounding of any area on the carving is accomplished, whether it be arms, legs tops of hats, or otherwise. You just keep shaving away sharp edges until the area is as round as you want it. I am going to stop at this point, as I prefer to leave some planes and facets on the wood. It gives more of a carved, rather than a 'molded' look.

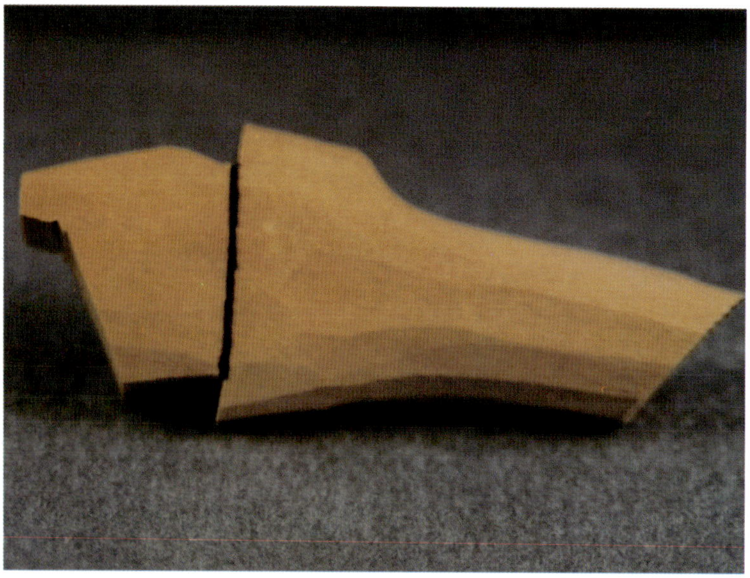

Sketch a line to define the separation between the end of the coat sleeve and the start of the hand (mitten). Do this on both sides of the arm.

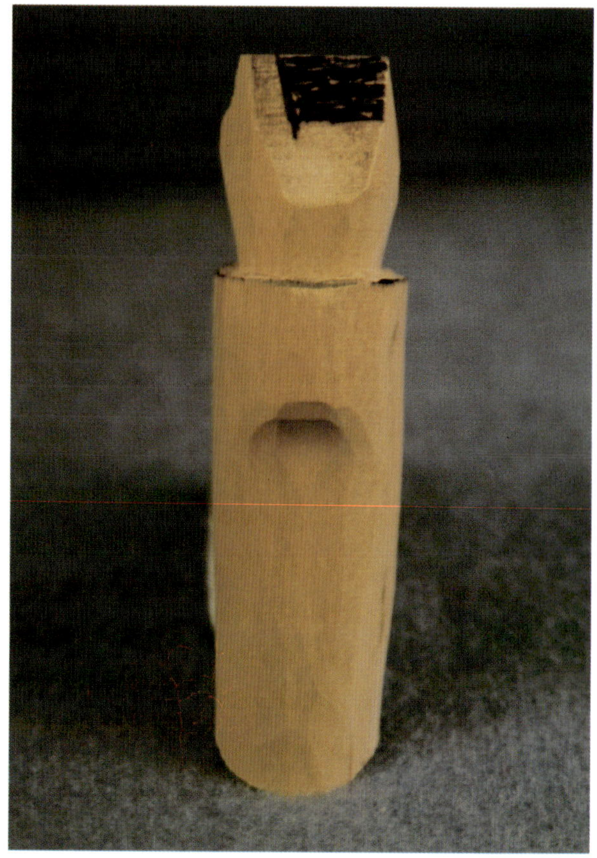

Using the tip of your knife, incise all the way around the mitten where it emerges from the sleeve, tracing over the line you sketched earlier. Shave away some wood, working from the mitten *toward* the end of the sleeve, to achieve this profile, as seen from the top. This forms a "wrist" area.

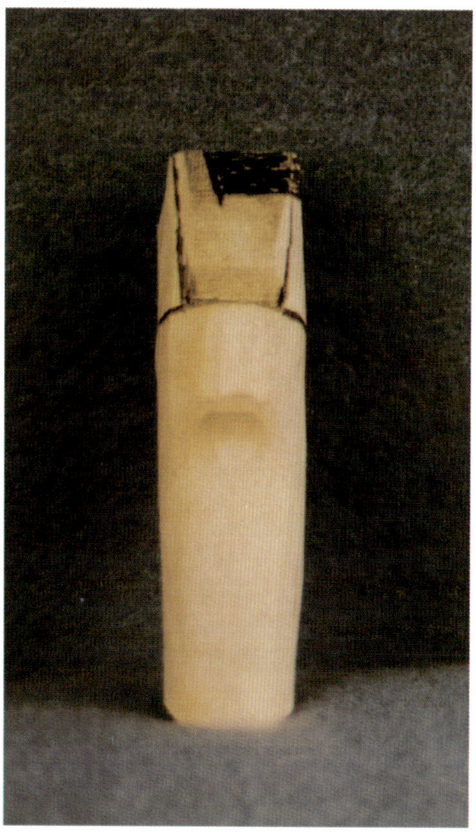

As viewed from the top, sketch in the top profile of the hand and thumb. The darkened wood will be removed as we shape the hand.

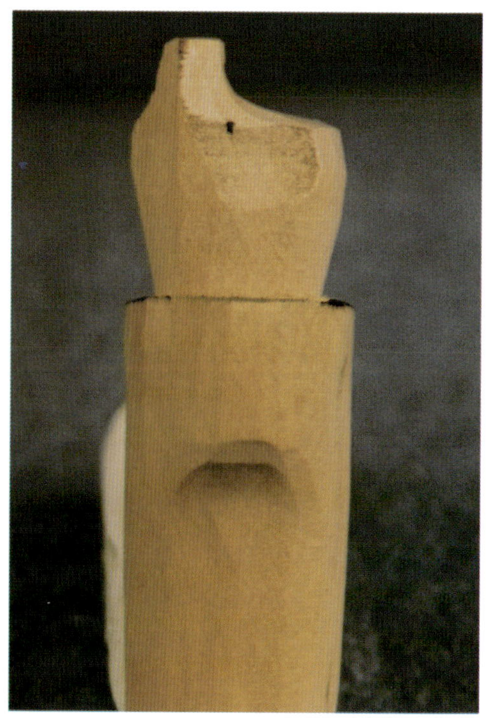

Still using your knife, shave away the darkened wood seen earlier to roughly form and define the thumb and hand area of the mitten, as seen from the top.

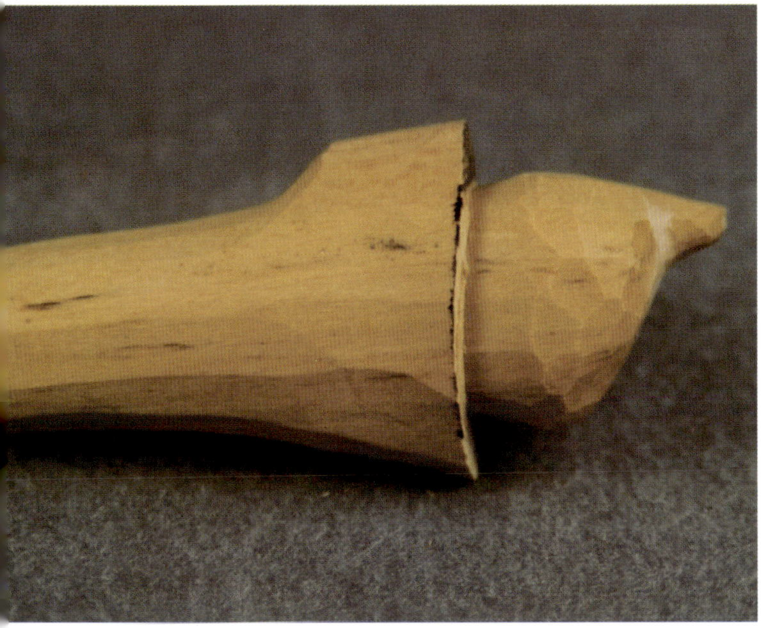

Continue using your knife to remove the sharp edges from the mitten, bringing it to a more rounded state. I like the way it looks at this point, so I am not going to do any more rounding.

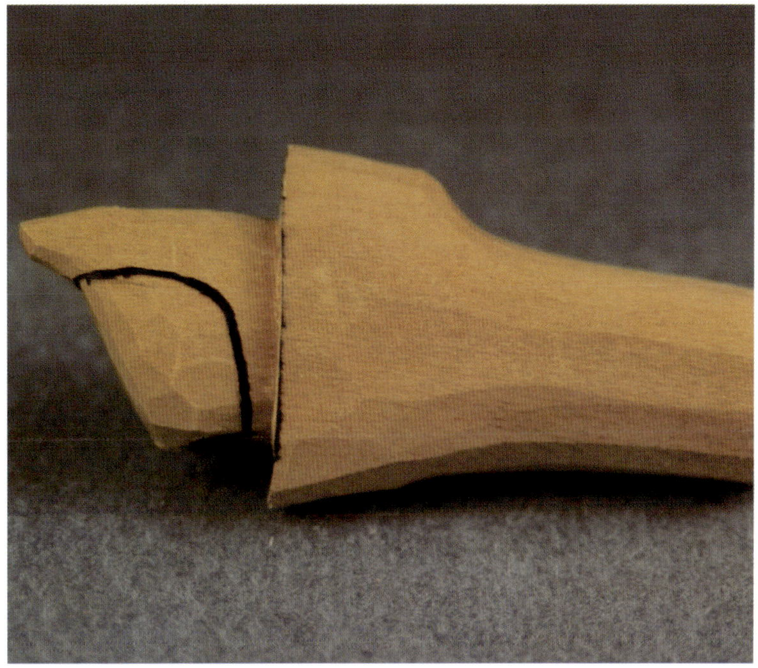

Sketch the inside portion of the thumb and hand section, as seen here.

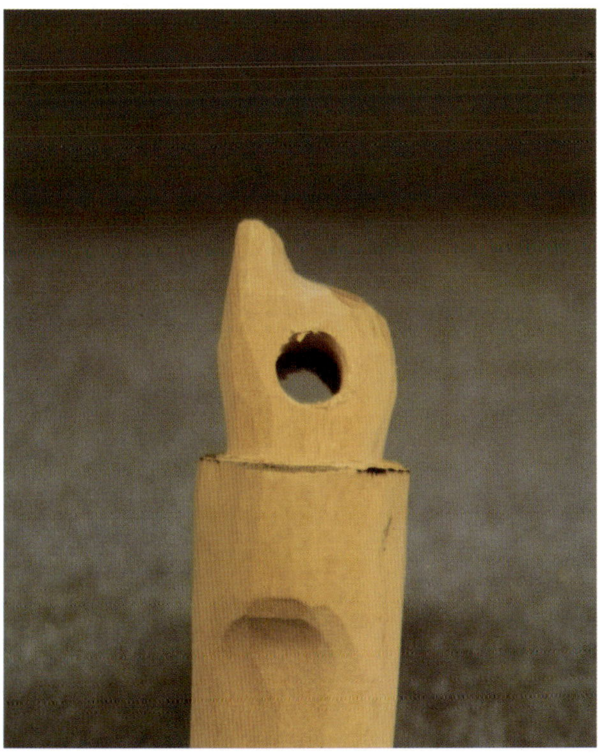

Now use a drill with a 1/4" bit to drill a hole all the way through the right hand, so it can hold a walking stick later. NOTE: be careful to try and follow the angle of the hand when drilling the holes. You want the walking stick and lantern to fit correctly when the project is assembled later.

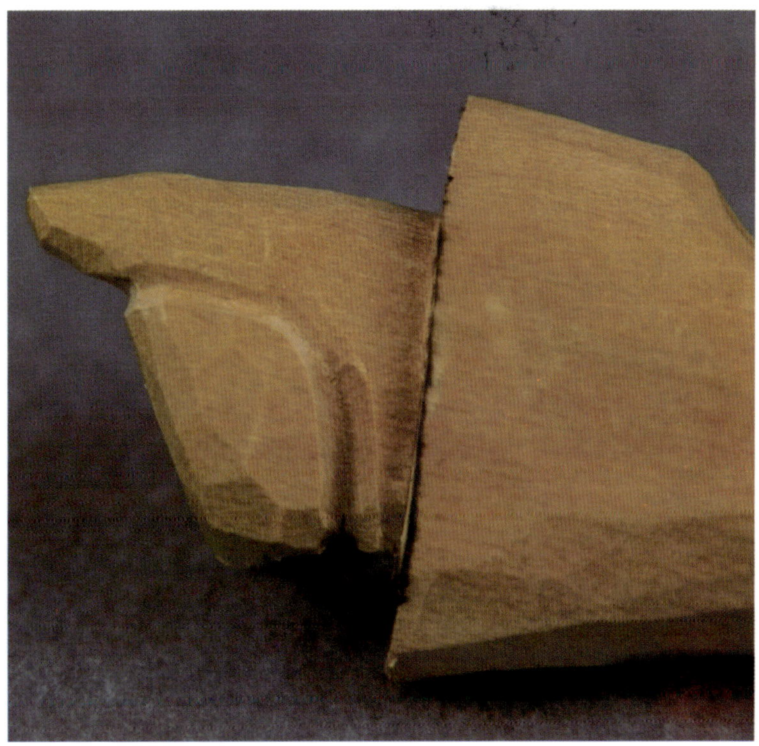

Use the tip of your knife or the 3mm V-gouge to incise the lines about 1/16" deep. Shave away wood from both sides of the incision to form a V-channel, as seen here. This will further define the thumb, and will separate the hand section from it.

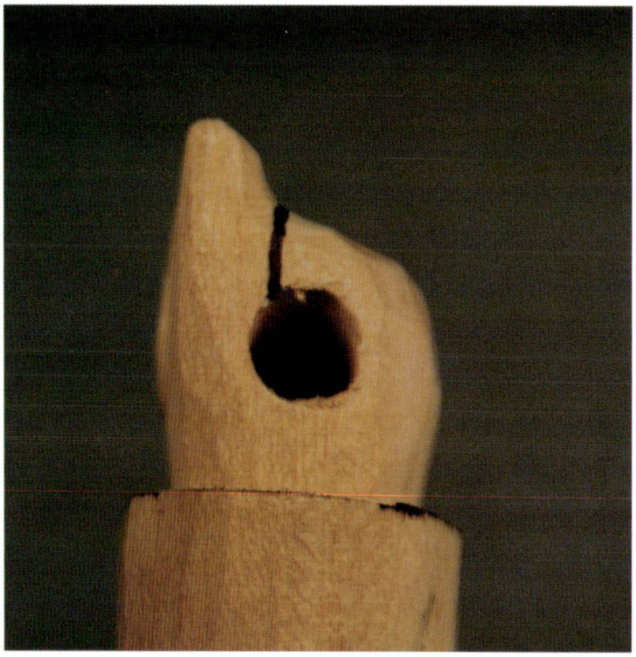

If necessary, sketch in a new line to define the thumb, as seen from the top. (It may still be there from a previous step if you didn't carve it away during the rounding process earlier).

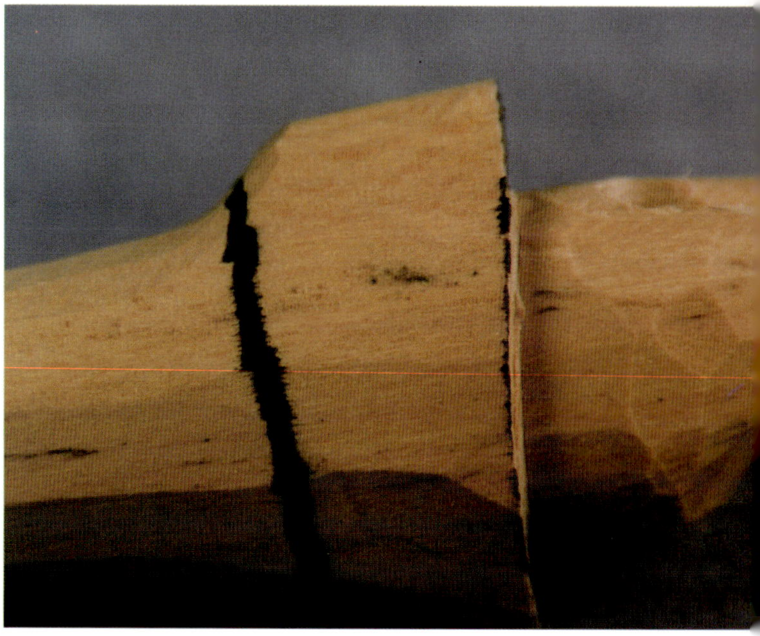

Sketch a line all around the arm to define the rear of the fur on the sleeve.

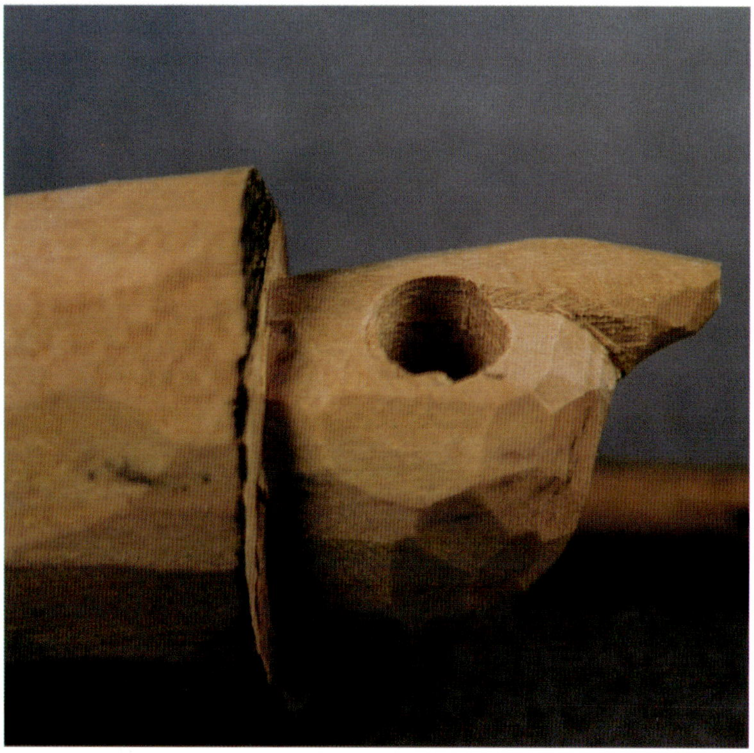

Incise the line with your knife tip. Shave away a small amount of wood so the hand area is slightly lower than the thumb. This just adds a bit more dimension and detail.

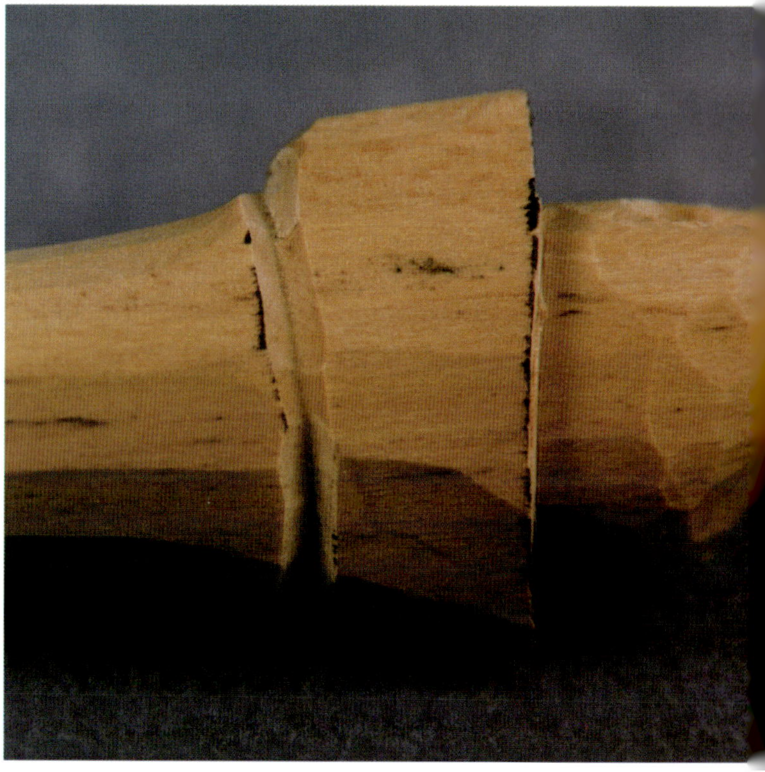

Use the 4.5 mm 60 degree V-gouge to trace over this line, all around the arm. This v-channel will separate the fur from the sleeve.

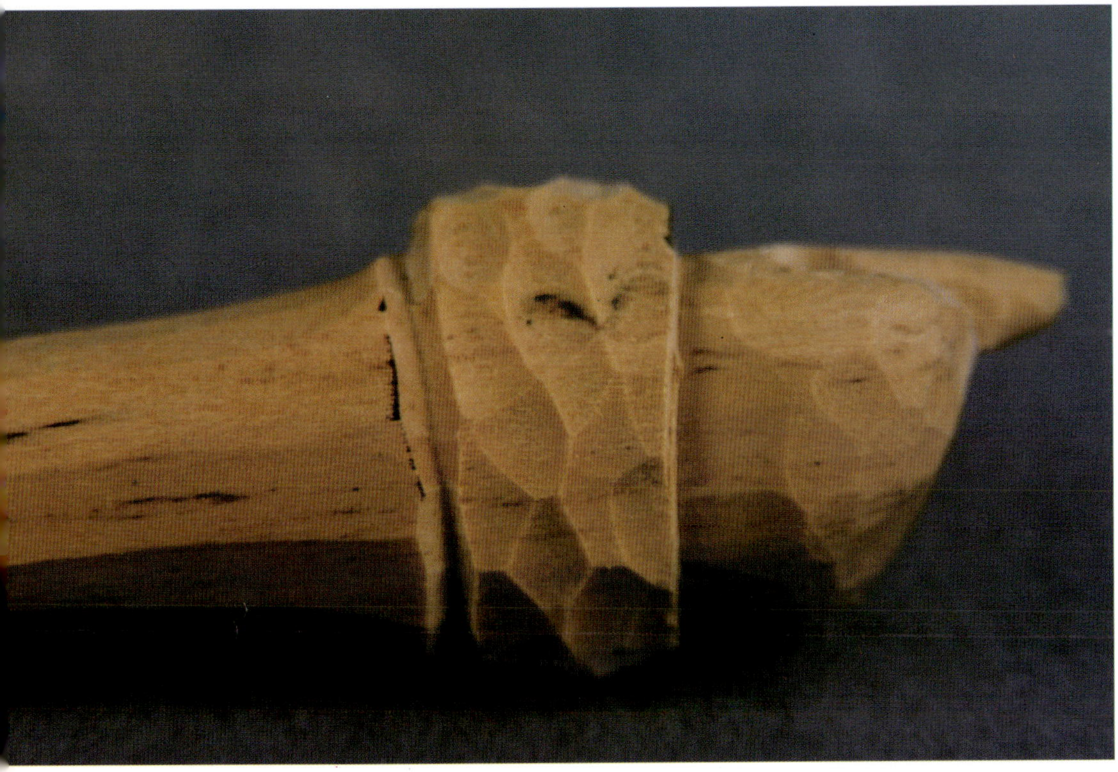

Add some 'detail' to the fur by scooping out random spots on the wood using the 6mm U-gouge to create lots of planes and facets. This gives a "whipped" effect to the flat surface of the wood, and after painting and antiquing, looks great. Any time you can use your gouges to break up flat areas of fur and hair, you should take the opportunity to do so. It increases the visual impact of you work tremendously, and removes much of the stiffness from the carving.

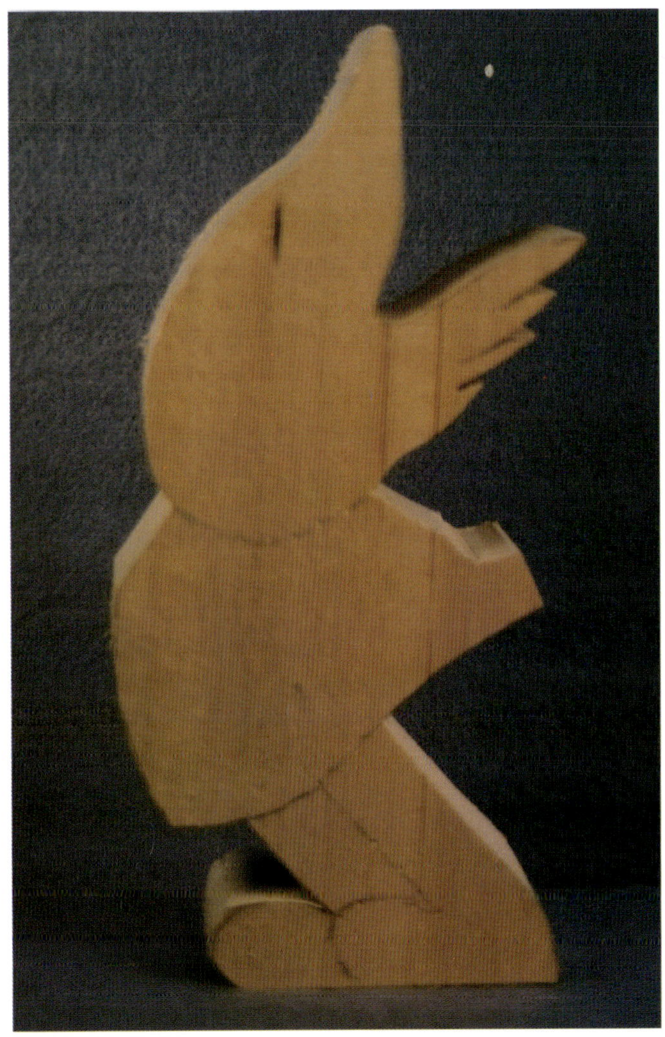

Transfer the body pattern to a piece of 1-3/4" or 2" thick wood, and saw it out.

Repeat this entire set of steps for the left hand and arm, and we'll be ready to use them to get us started carving the body of ol' santa. Use a 1/16" bit to drill a hole through the left hand so it can hold the lantern handle later.

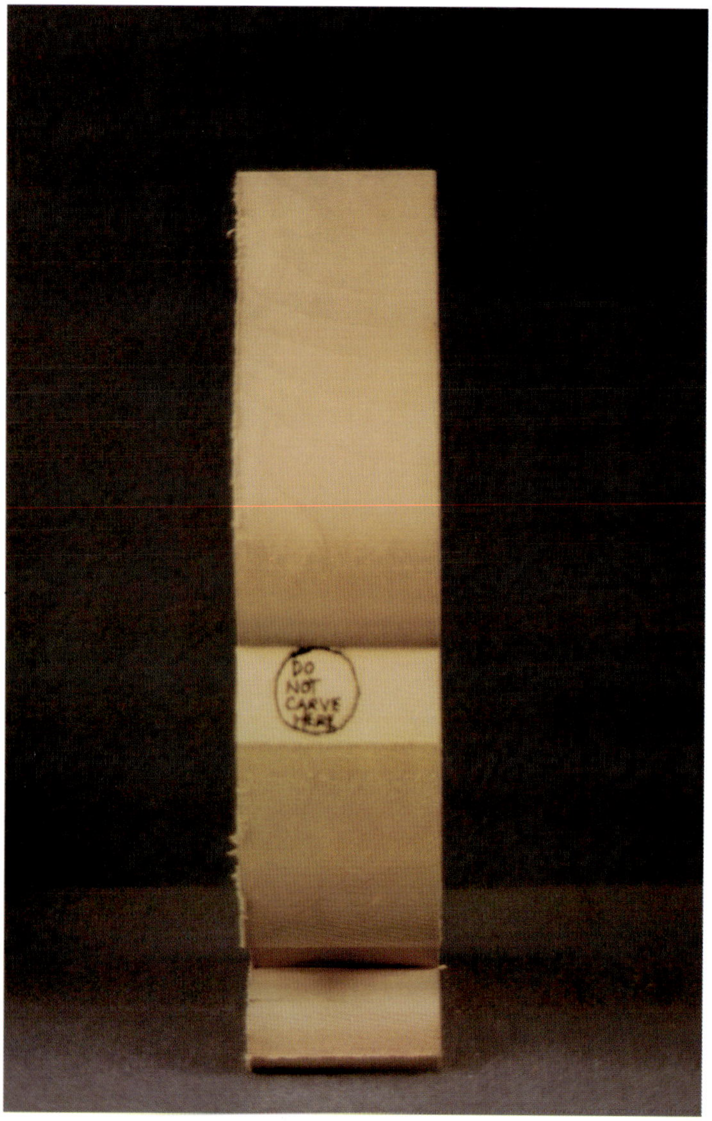

Place one arm against the body and trace around it where it makes contact with the body.

Use the pattern as a reference to get a rough idea where the arm should go. You are establishing a "no-carve" zone. This area within the circle must remain flat so the arm will fit flush to it later, when the components are assembled. After tracing the first arm, repeat this procedure for the other arm.

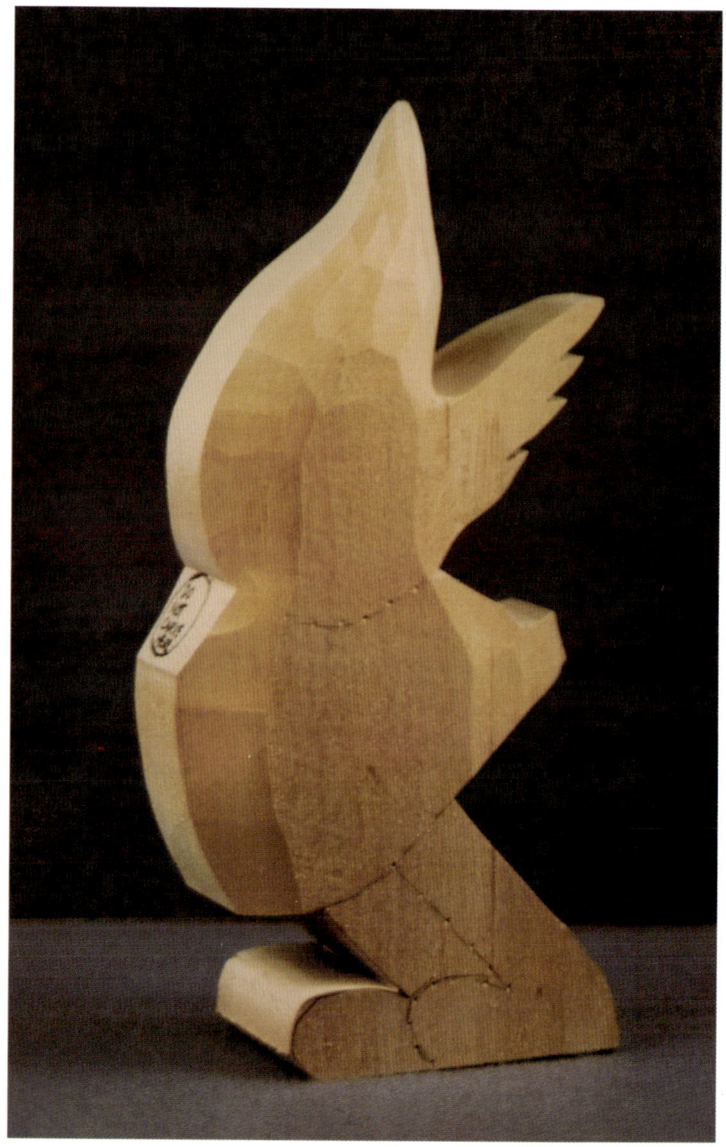

Set the arms aside for now (but don't lose them), and let's get busy on the body. Start by using your knife to knock off all four sharp edges from the body, working from the bottom of the coat up to the top of the hat. Stay away from the legs and feet for now - we'll work on them later. Exercise caution not to carve into the circled "no-carve" areas! (We'll clean up around them after the arms are glued in place later).

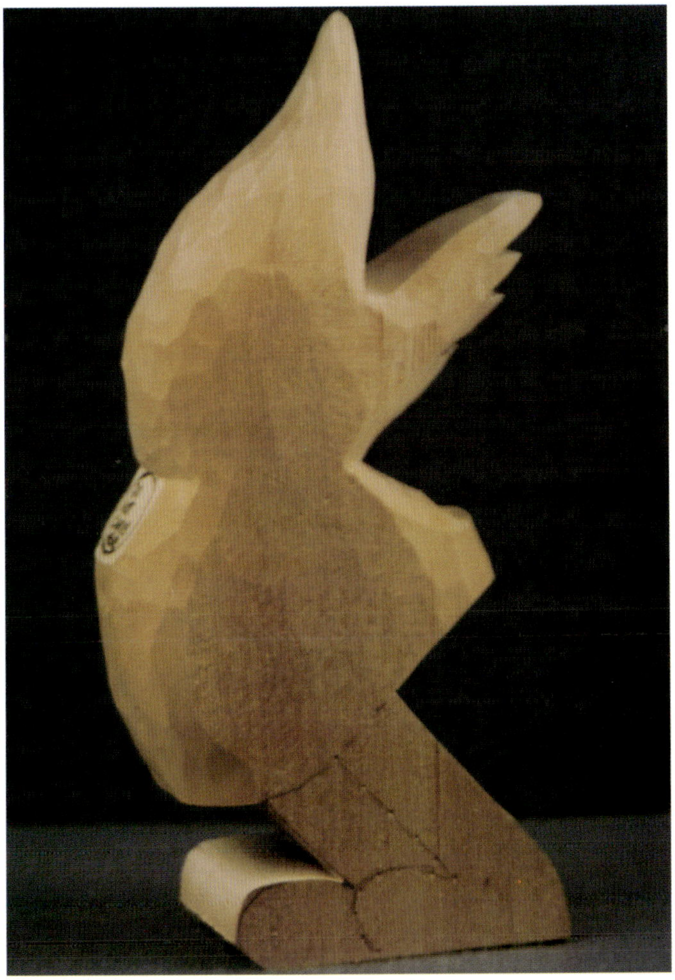

Continue rounding on the main body (but not legs and feet!), using your knife. We are attempting to get as much general shaping as possible accomplished, before getting into the detail carving. This process also removes the outer layer of wood, which opens up the pores and helps it to more readily accept the paint stain later.

Now we can start roughing-in the details. Sketch a line as shown to define the bottom of the beard in front.

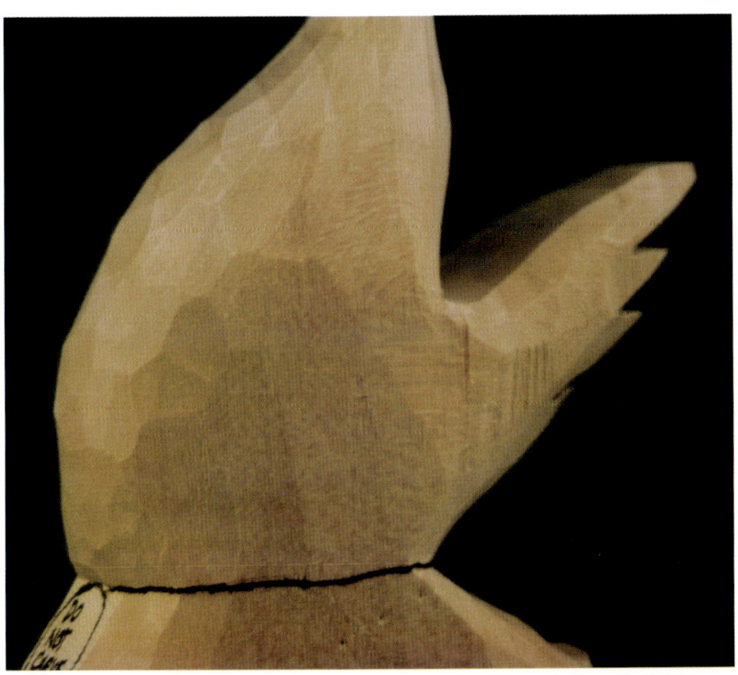

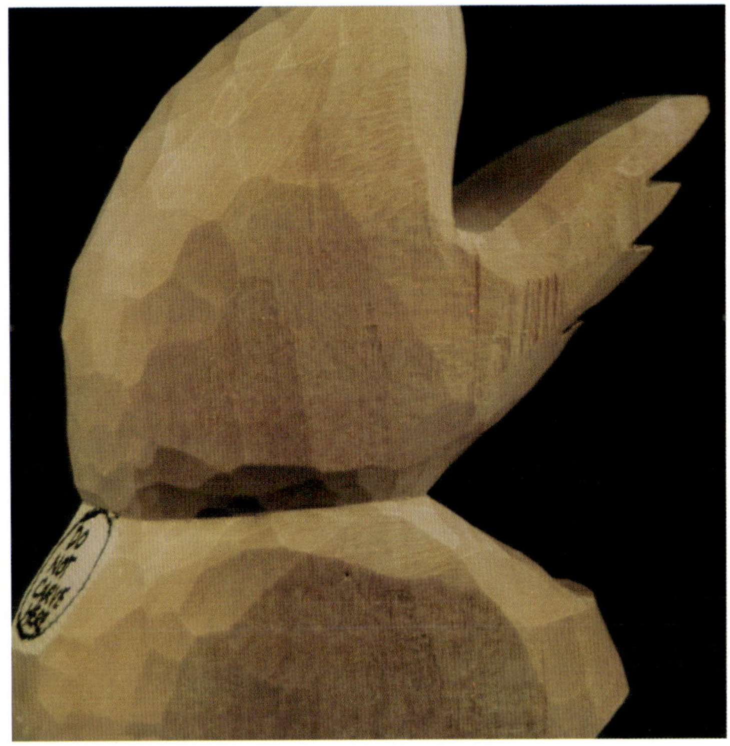

Incise the line with your knife tip. Then working from the body up toward the line you incised, and down from the beard, remove wood from the coat using your knife or a #1 10mm straight gouge. This will make the coat slightly lower than the beard, making the beard stand out.

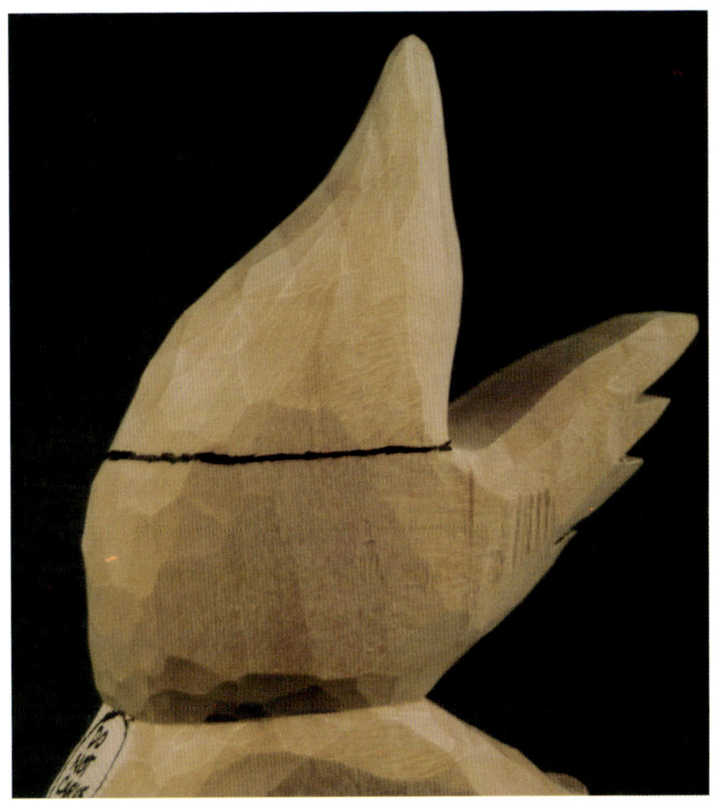

Sketch in the bottom of the hat, as shown here, all around the head.

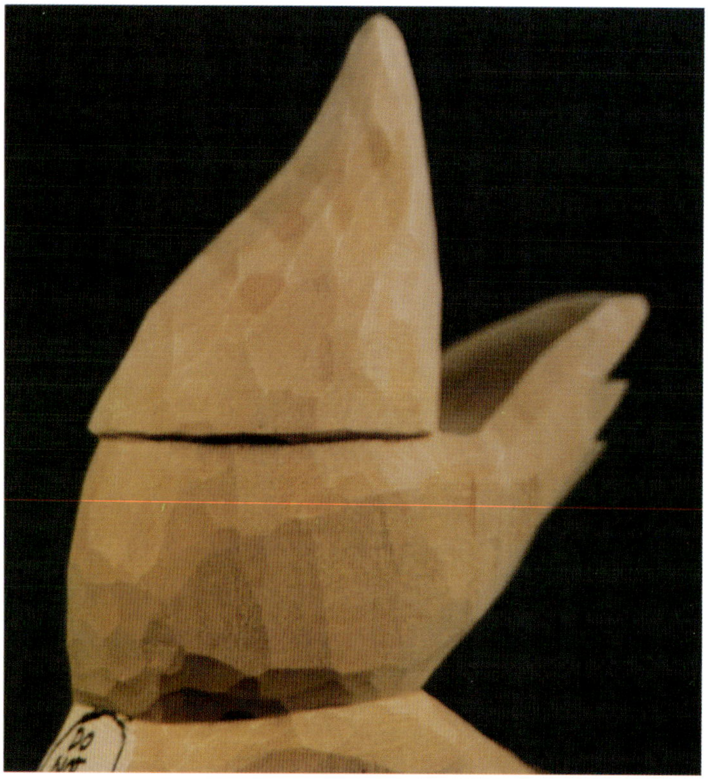

Incise the line with your knife tip or trace over it using a #39 4.5mm V-gouge. Then, working from the face up toward the bottom of the hat, use your knife to remove a small amount of wood so the hat stands out from the face and beard as seen here in front.....

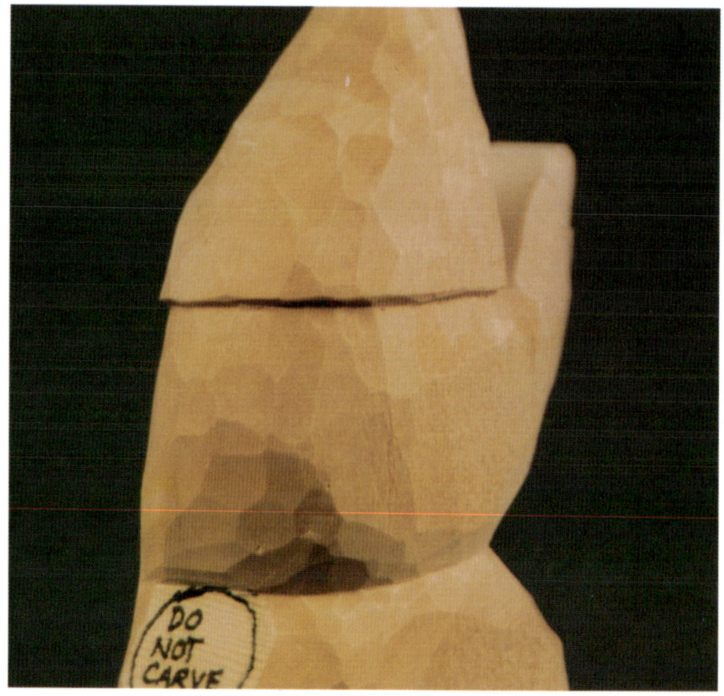

Use your knife to finish rounding and shaping the hat. Once the hat shape is established, we'll know how much excess beard to remove from the rear of the head.

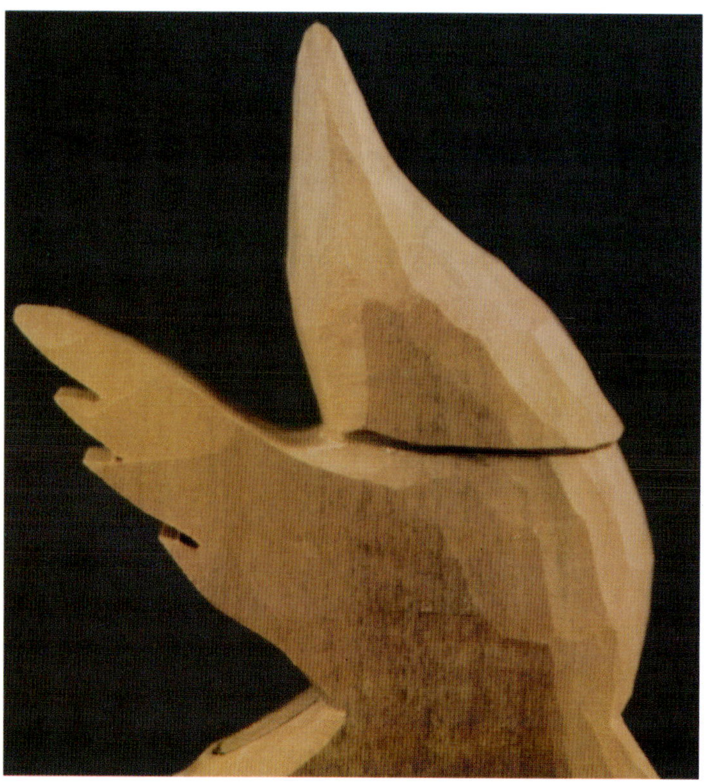

And here in the back.

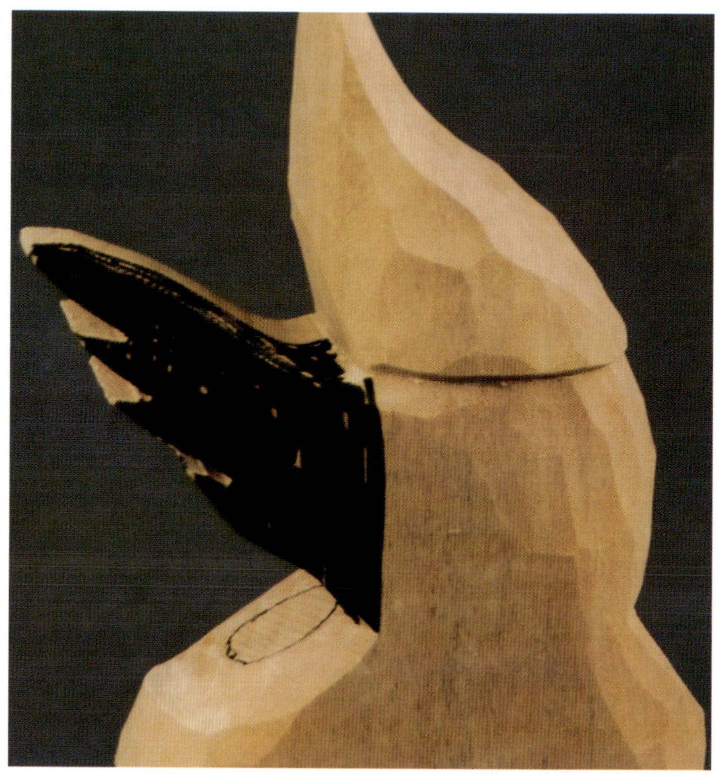

In this view, I have darkened the excess wood I will remove, using my knife and #1 10mm straight gouge. Once this wood is removed, I will be able to define the back of the hair, where it contacts the coat. Use care here, as the grain is running vertically through the beard.

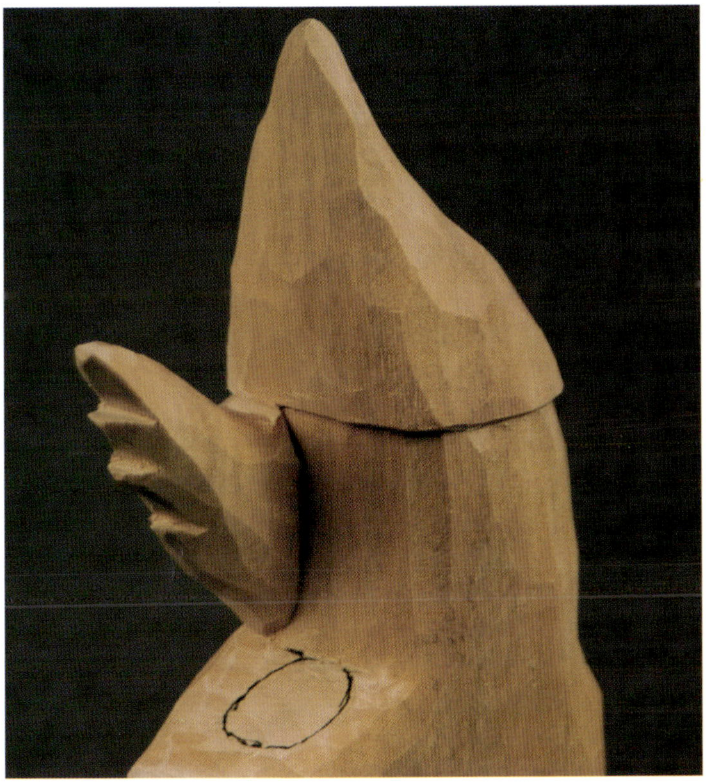

And here is the result, once the darkened wood has been removed.

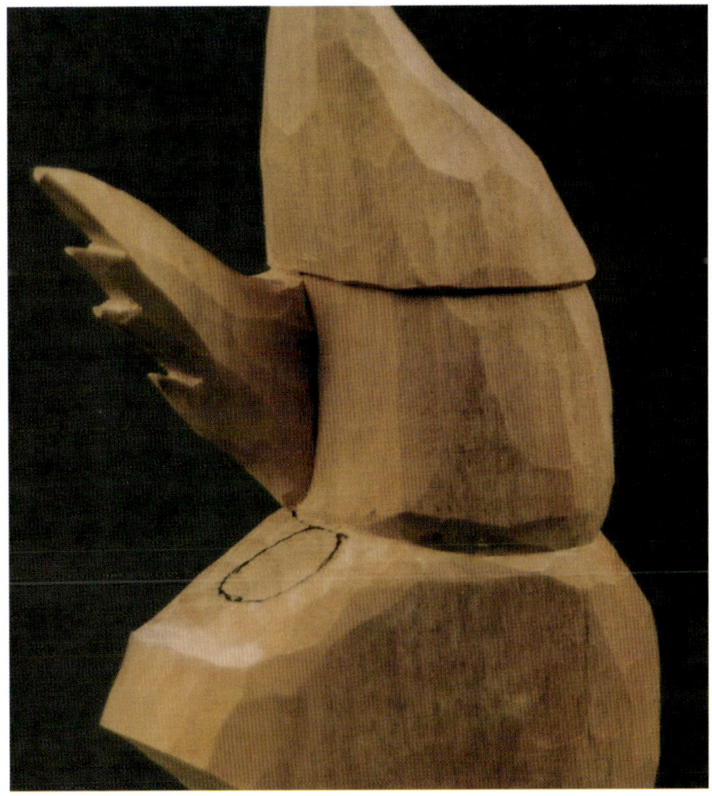

Using your knife or #39 4.5mm V-gouge, remove wood along this line so a V-groove is formed. This will separate the hair from the coat.

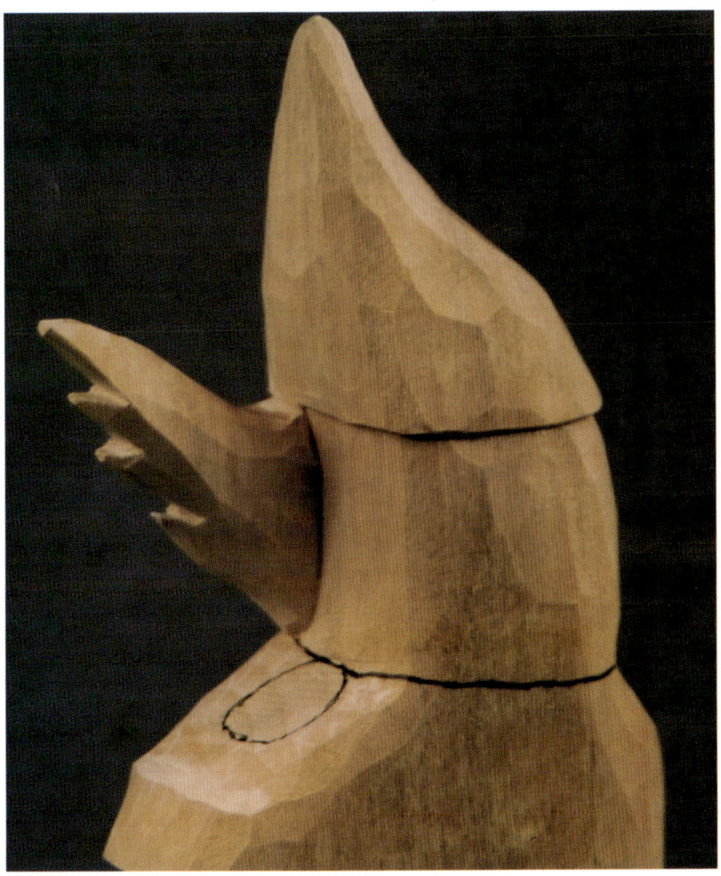

Now, sketch a line to define where the hair contacts the coat, all the way around the side and back of the head.

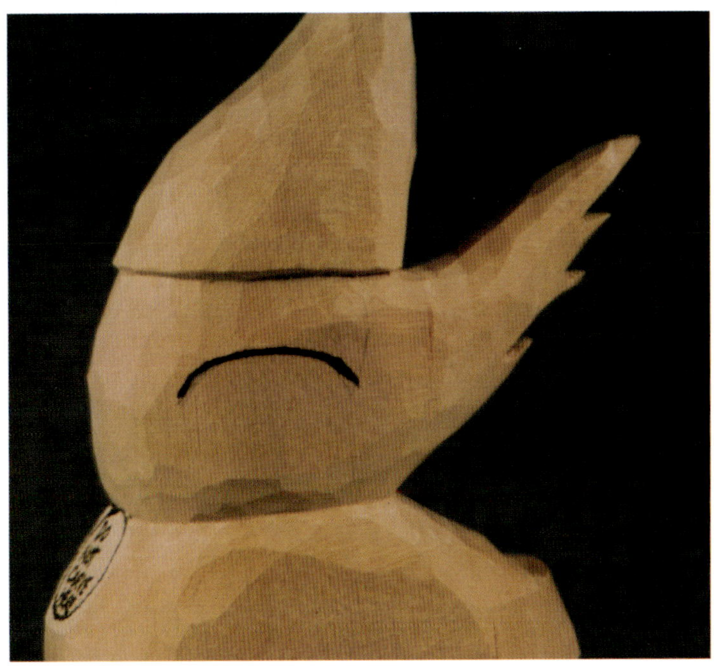

Now let's get a face on this ol' rascal. We are going to do this using one of Uncle Al's E-Z santa face techniques. Identify where you want the top of the cheeks to be. (This will change from carving to carving, at your option and as dictated by the amount of wood area you have for the face). Sketch in a curved line as seen here to establish the initial definition for the top of the cheeks, so we can get an idea where to locate the eyes.

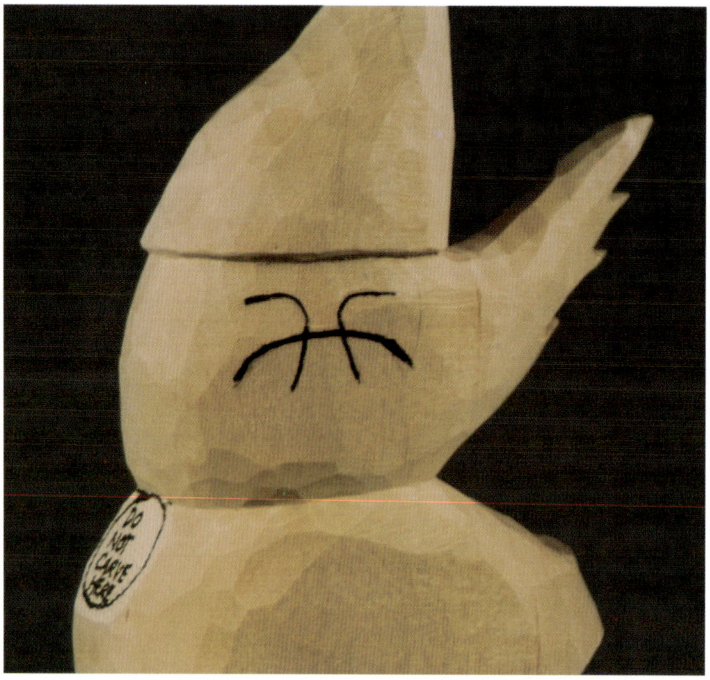

Next, sketch in two lines up the middle of the face and curving out, as seen here. These define the sides of the nose, and the top of the eye area. This is yet another area you can change from carving to carving, in order to achieve many different facial expressions. (Wide nose, thin nose, big eyes, small eyes, etc.).

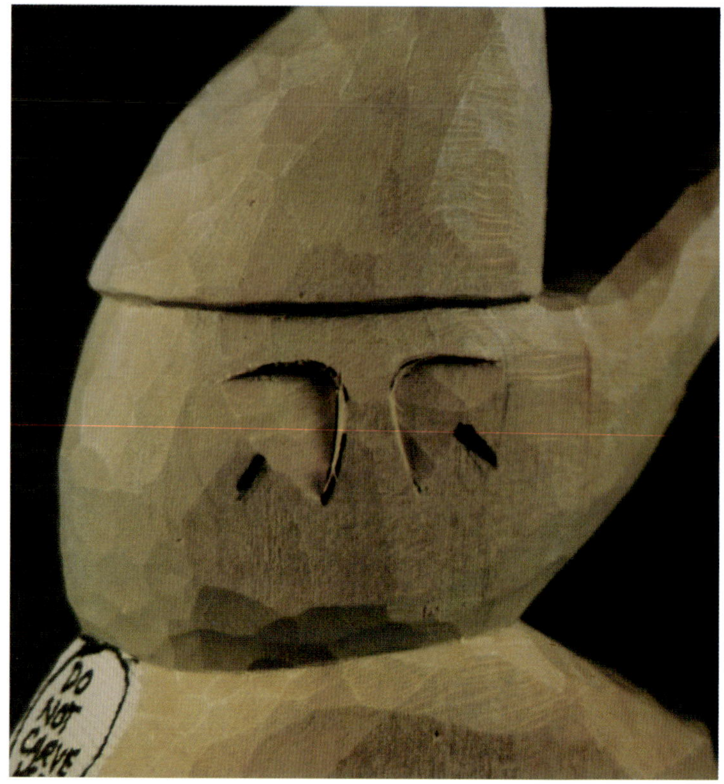

Using your knife, shave away a small amount of wood from both sides of the nose and under the curved eye lines, so the nose stands out from the main face area, and the eye socket is formed

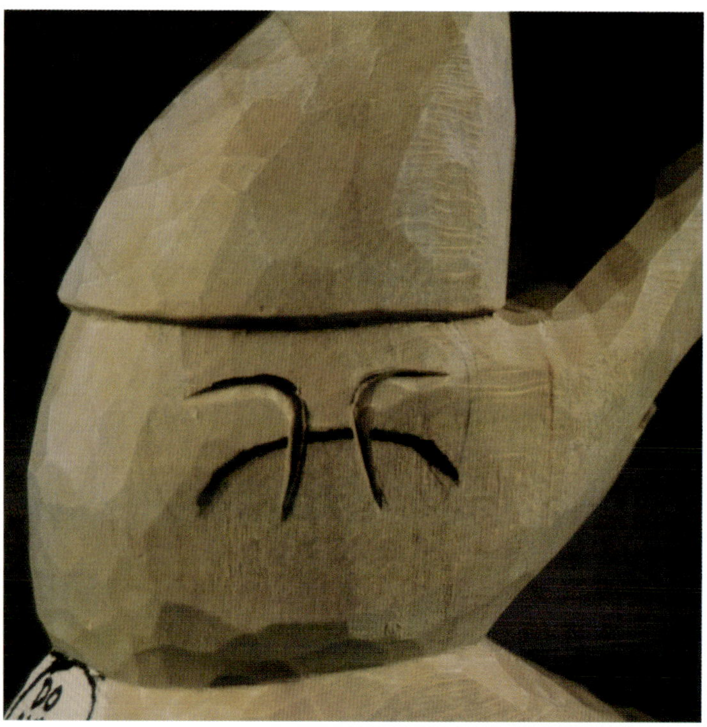

Using your knife tip, with the knife slanting in toward the center of the face, incise the nose/eye lines about 1/8" deep. Then, with the knife slanting toward the outside edges of the face, go over the lines again. This should release a v-shaped sliver of wood, as seen here. The nose is starting to appear, and you have a good start on the eye sockets.

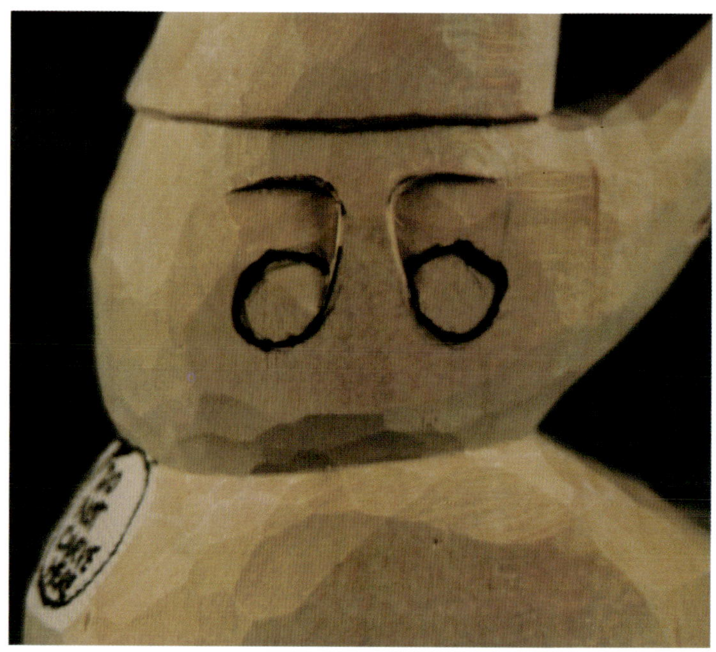

If the initial cheek line you drew is now gone because of the previous step, re-establish the curved cheek line you first drew, on both sides of the nose.

Then, on both sides of the nose , and using the cheek lines you just drew, complete these lines by turning them into circles, as seen here. These will serve as rough approximations of where the full cheeks will be later, while you are working on the nose.

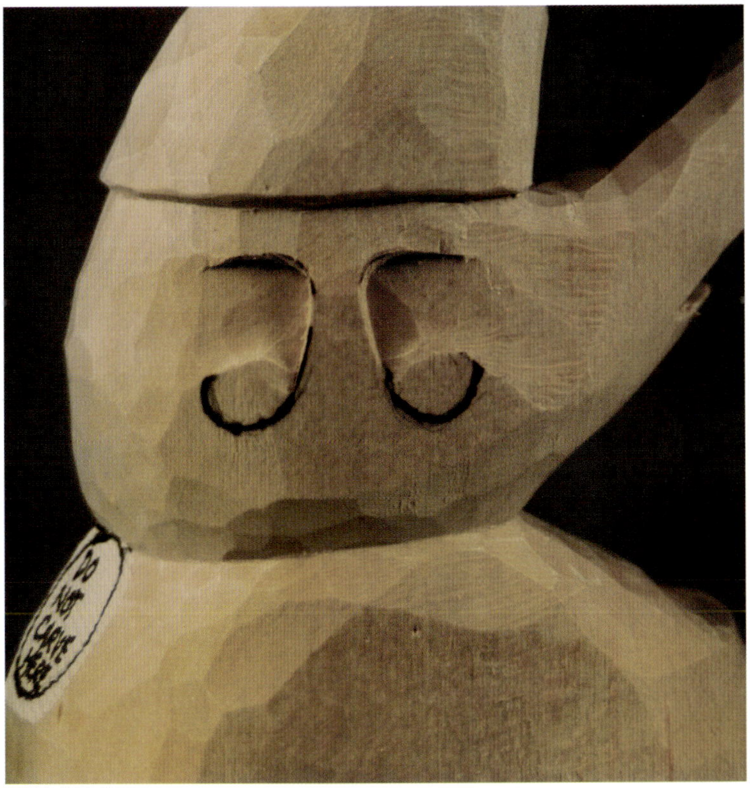

Using an in-and-up motion with your knife (a "scooping" motion), remove some wood as shown, so the upper part of the face becomes recessed from the cheek tops. This is another area you can vary from carving to carving to give different cheek effects. Round off the top edges of the cheeks, if necessary, so they blend smoothly into the upper face area.

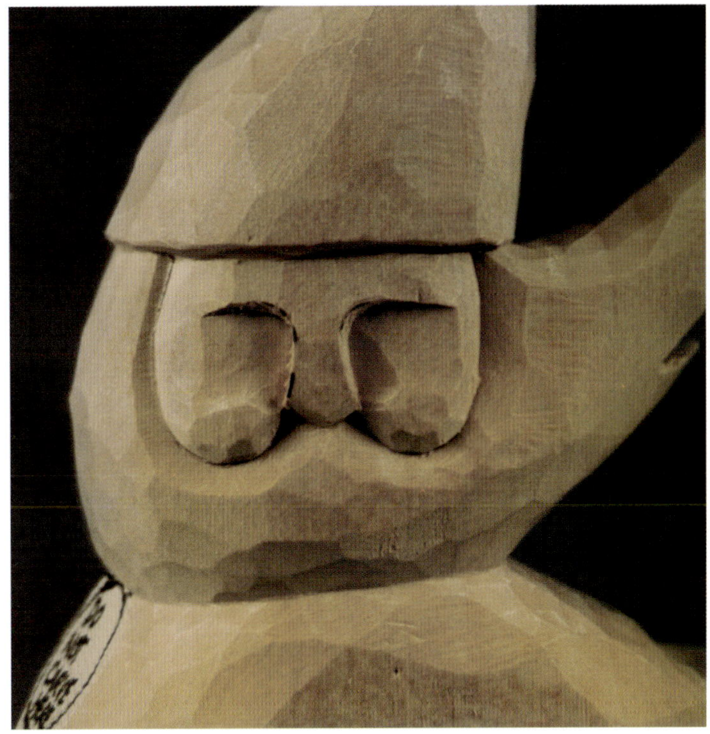

Using the tip of your knife, incise these lines about 1/8" deep.

Following these lines with your knife, shave downward toward them from the top of the face, and then upward from the bottom of the face, so a 'v' channel is formed. Now we have the face and nose defined, and separated from the beard.

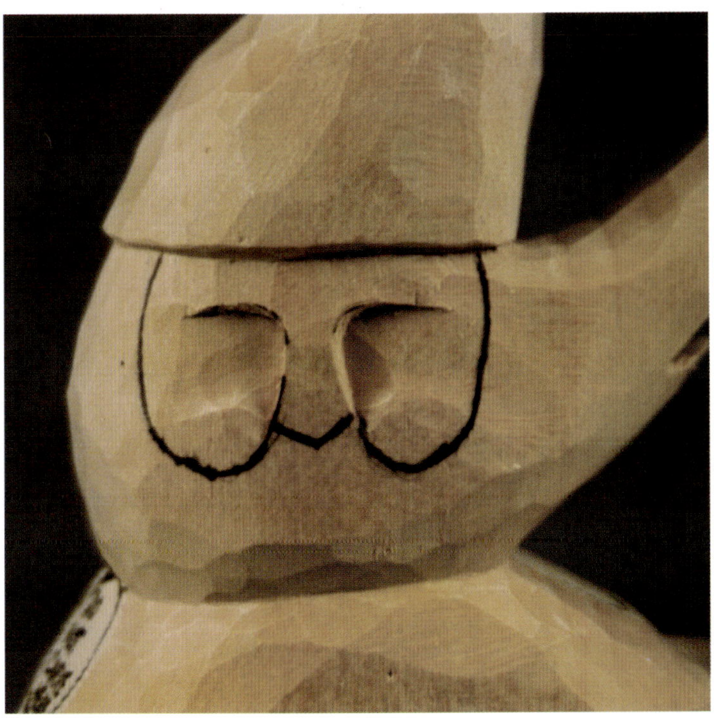

Sketch in lines to continue the cheek bottoms around and up the sides of the face. Also, sketch in the bottom of the nose. Notice that I have sketched angle lines on the nose bottom. These will be rounded off as we progress.

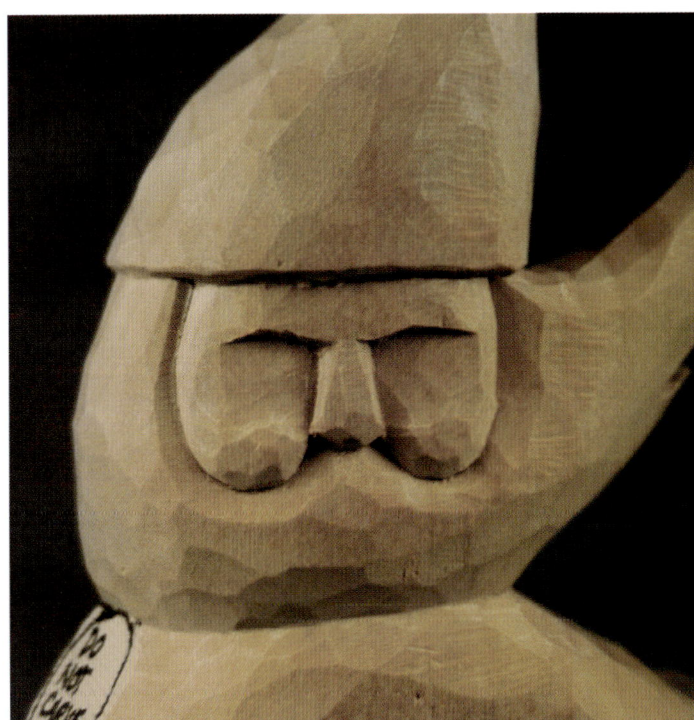

Use your knife or #1 10mm straight gouge to remove the sharp edges from the nose where we separated it from the cheeks and face. Also, use your knife to nip off the bottom of the nose, and round off any sharp edges that were created.

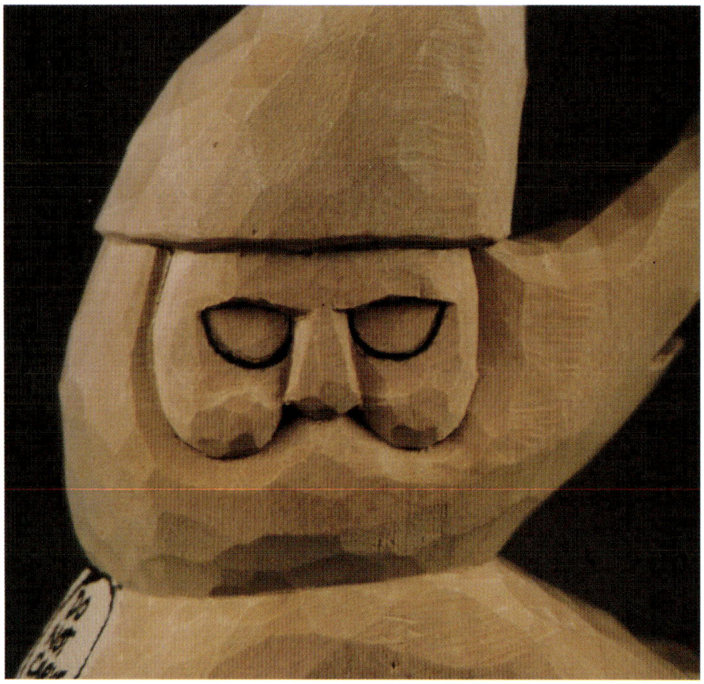

Now, sketch in the two eyes, as seen here. Yes, this is another variable you can change from one carving to the next. Are you starting to see how you could get an endless number of facial expressions from using just one pattern as a basic starting point?

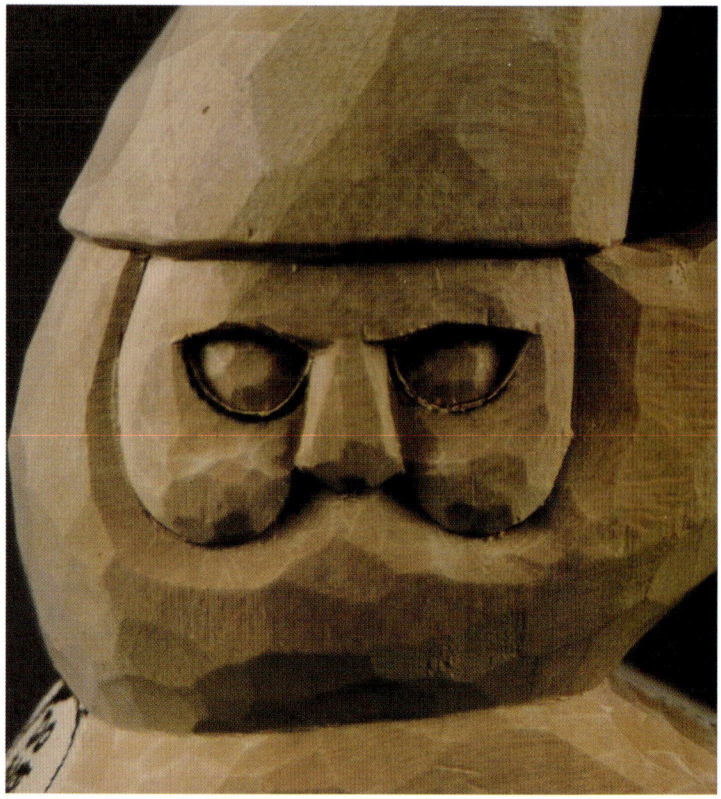

Now, go around the edges of the eyeballs with your knife and remove a small amount of wood. This will give them a slightly rounded effect, as seen here.

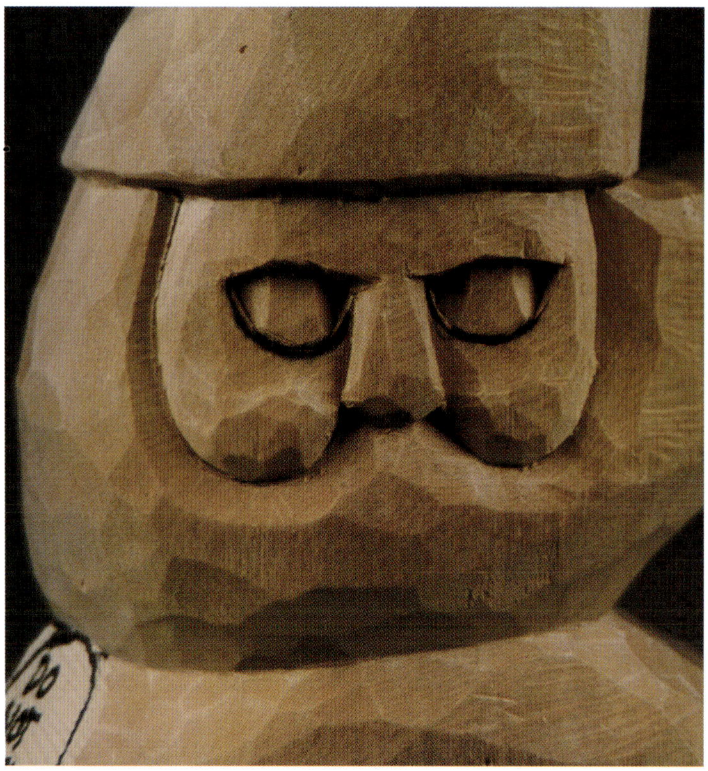

Use your knife tip to trace over these lines, incising about 1/16" deep. Remove wood from the corners of the eyes, at about a 45 degree angle. If you incised deep enough and clean enough (here is where a dull knife will tell on you), when you make the angle cuts in the corners, the wood should just fall out.

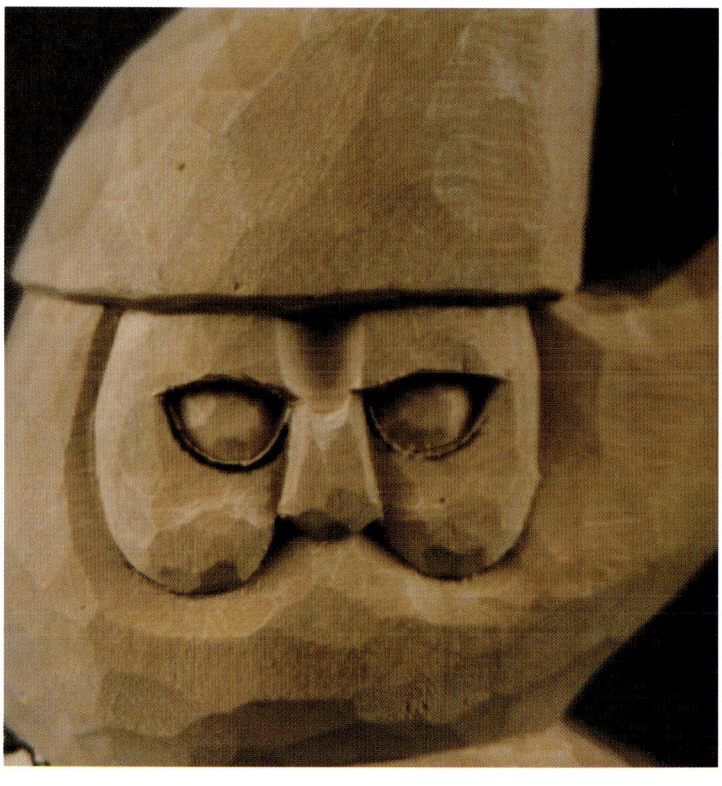

To get the eyebrows defined, first use the #9 4.5mm U-gouge to cut a groove up the center of the face, above the nose, centered between the eyes.

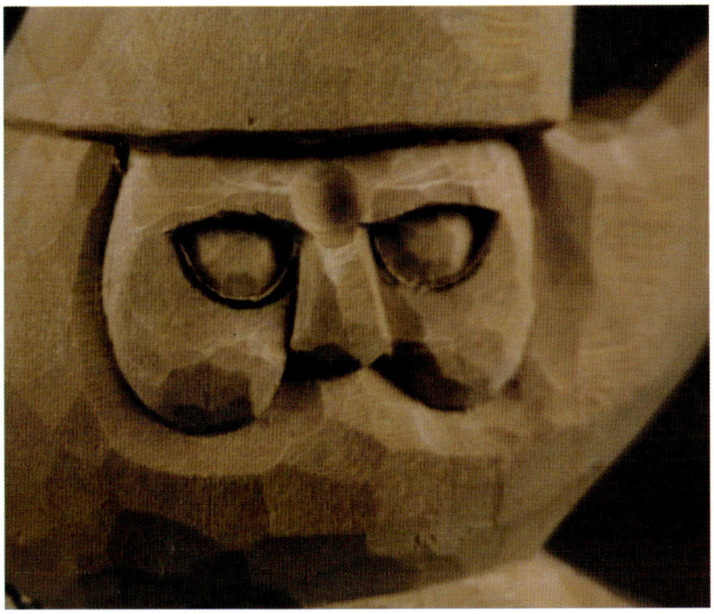

Now, with your tried-and-true scooping method, use your knife to remove some wood from the tops of the eyebrows, so they stand out from the face.

I'm happy with the main face details at this point, so I'll quit before I get into trouble, and get back to work on the beard. A good rule to live by: when you reach a point on your carving where you are satisfied, stop! Many times, when you go in and decide to "tweak" an area just a little bit more, you suddenly and sadly discover that you should have left it alone. If you don't like the way it looks, do it differently the next time.

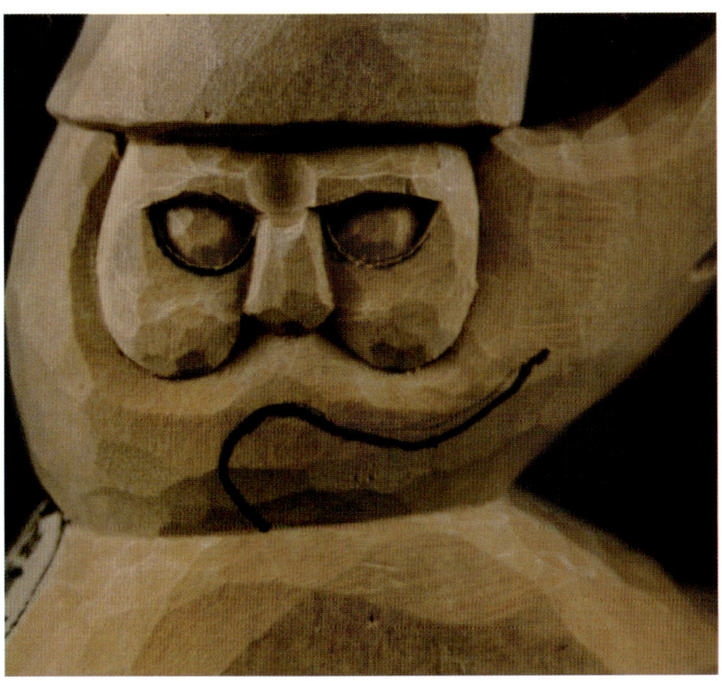

Sketch in a curved line to define the wind-blown mustache. Again, here is another variable you can change from carving to carving, so all your faces have a different 'personality'.

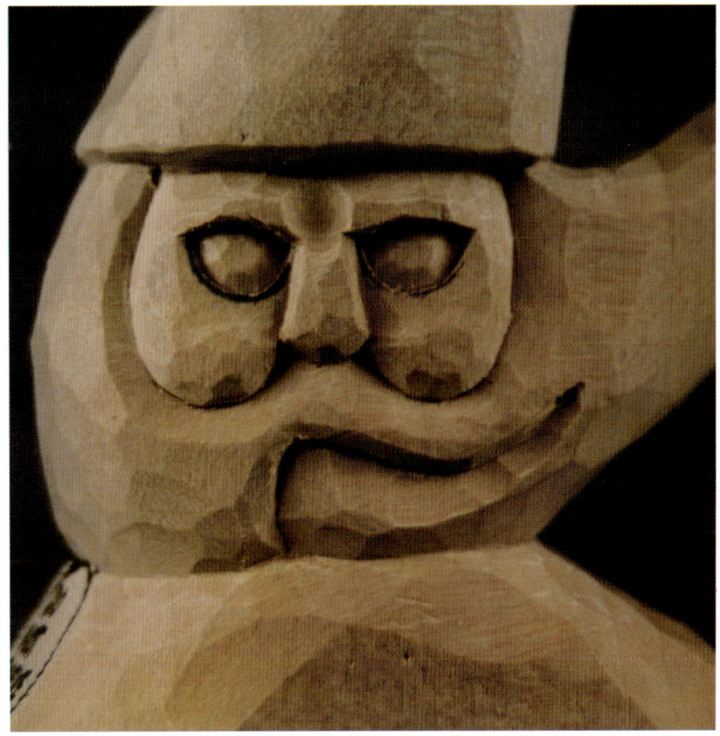

Incise the line with your knife tip about 1/8" deep. Using your knife, shave down toward the line from the top of the mustache, and up from the beard, so a small amount of wood is removed under the mustache. This will make the mustache stand out from the beard.

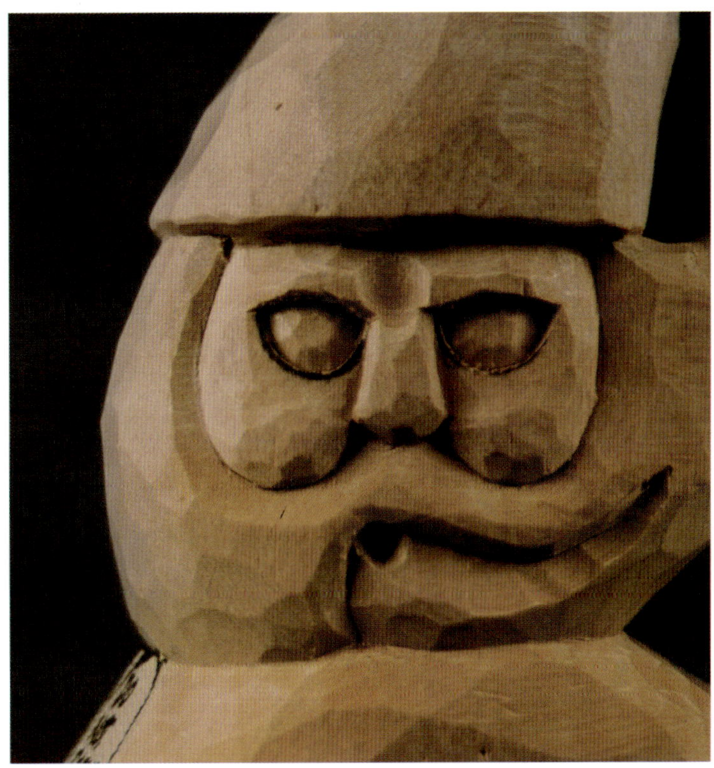

Using a 1/8" nail-set, or drill bit, make a mouth hole at the inside top of the mustache.

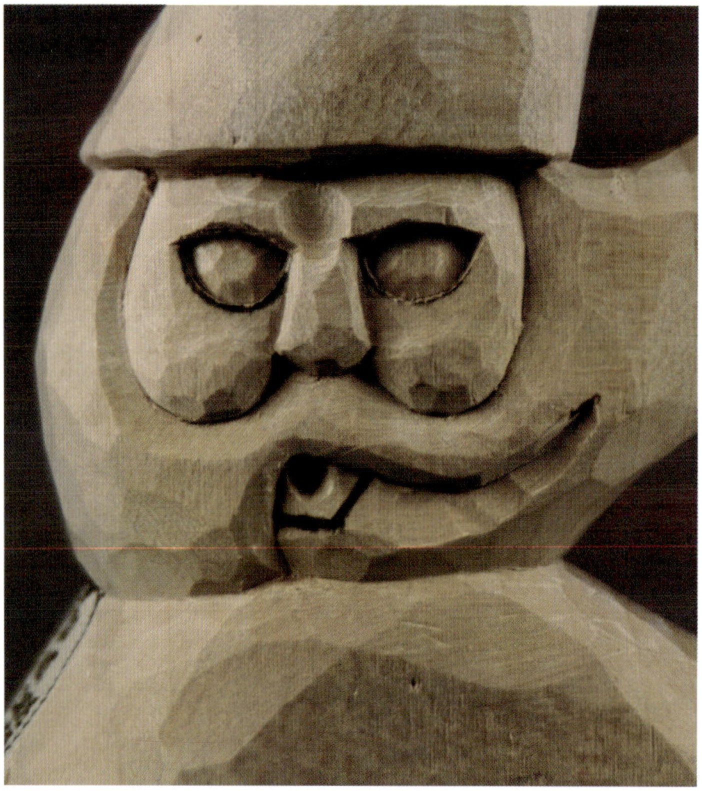

Sketch in the lower lip. (*Another* variable!)

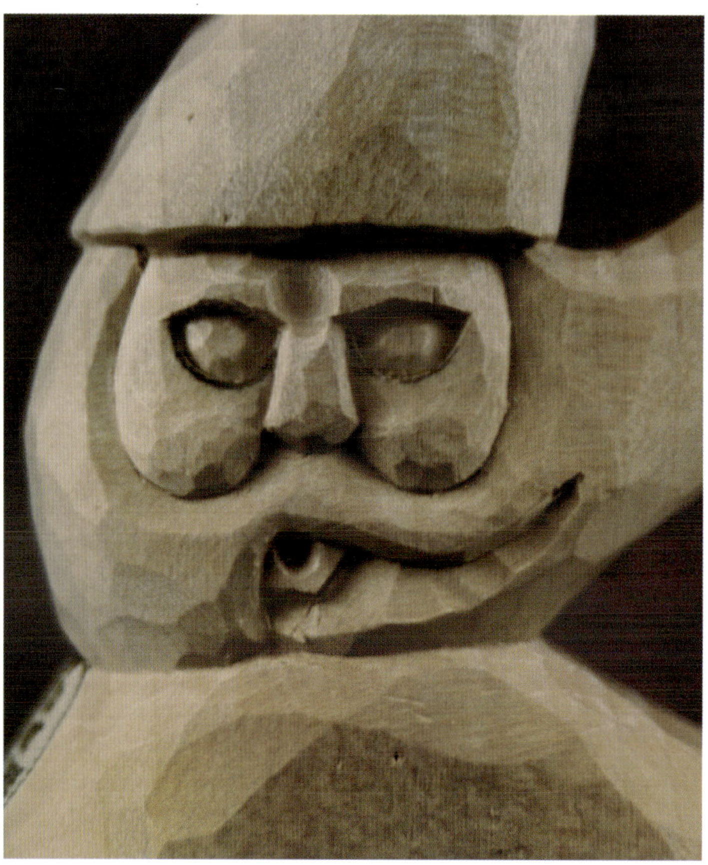

Incise the lip lines about 1/16" deep with your knife tip , then shave away a small amount of wood below the lines, in order to make the lip stand out.

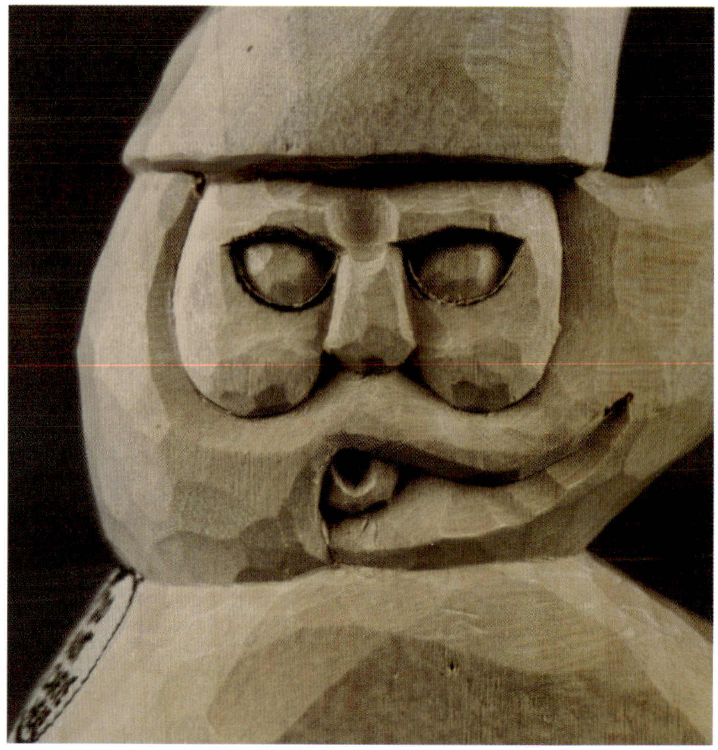

Nip off the bottom point of the lip with your knife, round off the sharp edges, and the lip is done.

Use the #9 4.5mm U-gouge and #9 6mm U-gouge to add details to the mustache, beard and hair. For extra effect (optional), you can then use the #39 4.5mm V-gouge to cut in a few more details into the beard. You may be bold and daring and also use a gouge to add texture to the eyebrows. If you don't do this, your Santa will still look just fine.

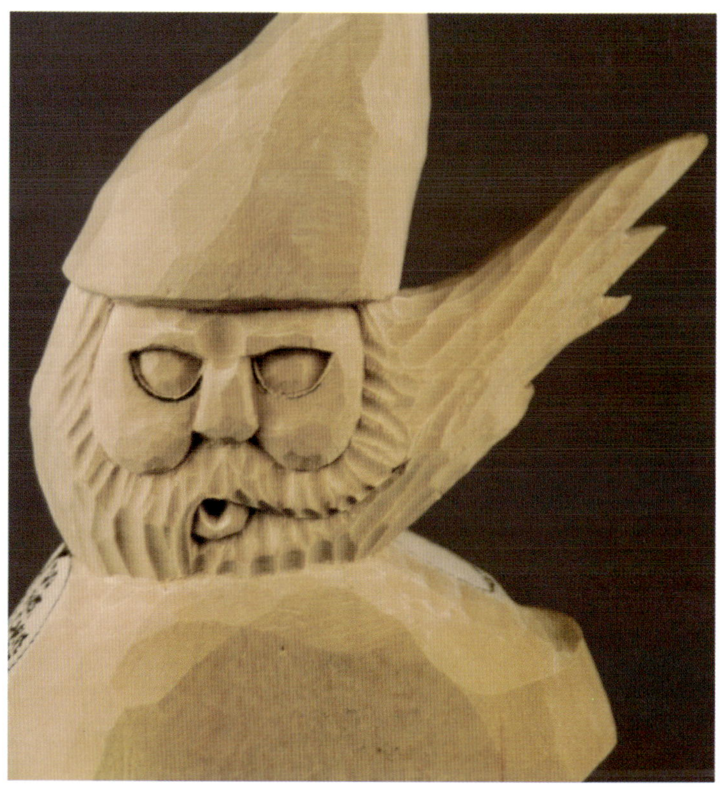

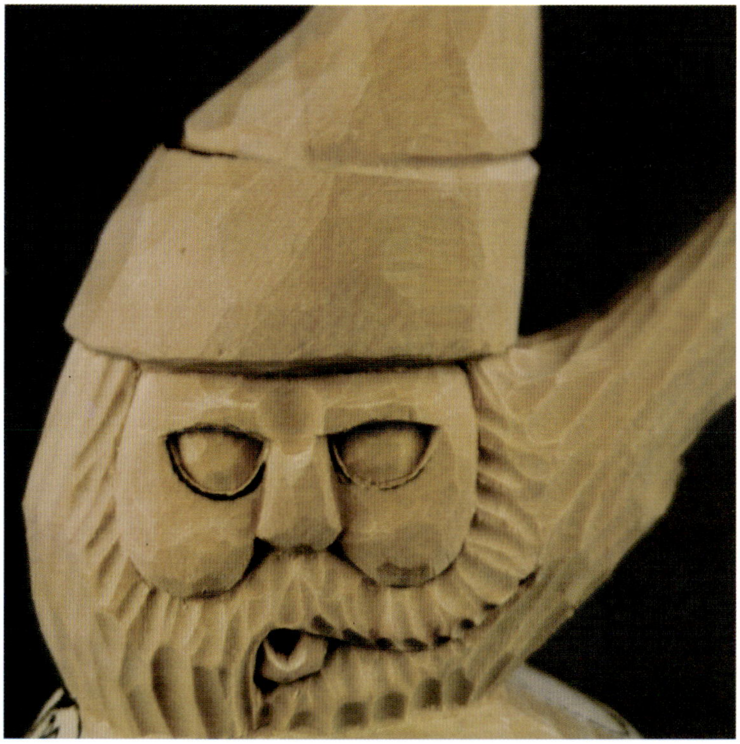

Now that the face, beard and hair are done, let's finish the hat.

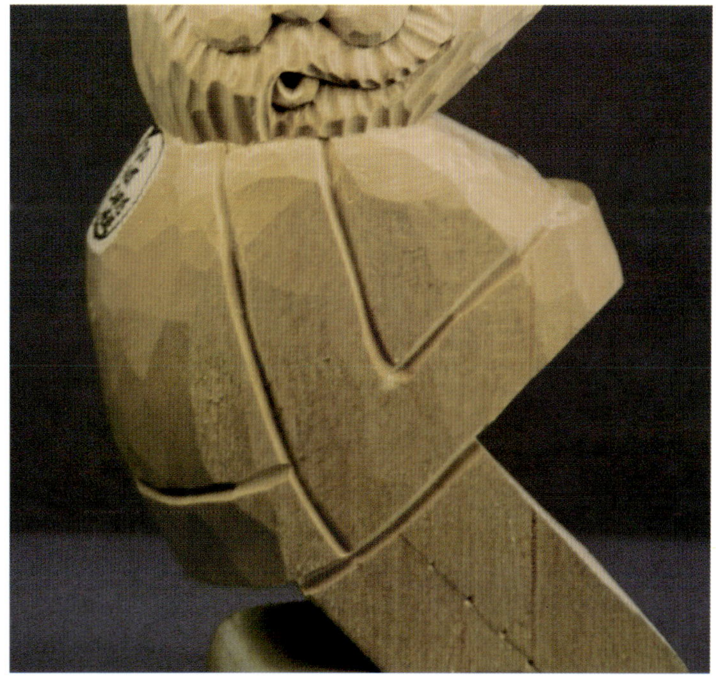

Sketch in the fur lines on the coat all the way around. Using the #39 4.5mm V-gouge, trace over these lines to remove wood in front.....

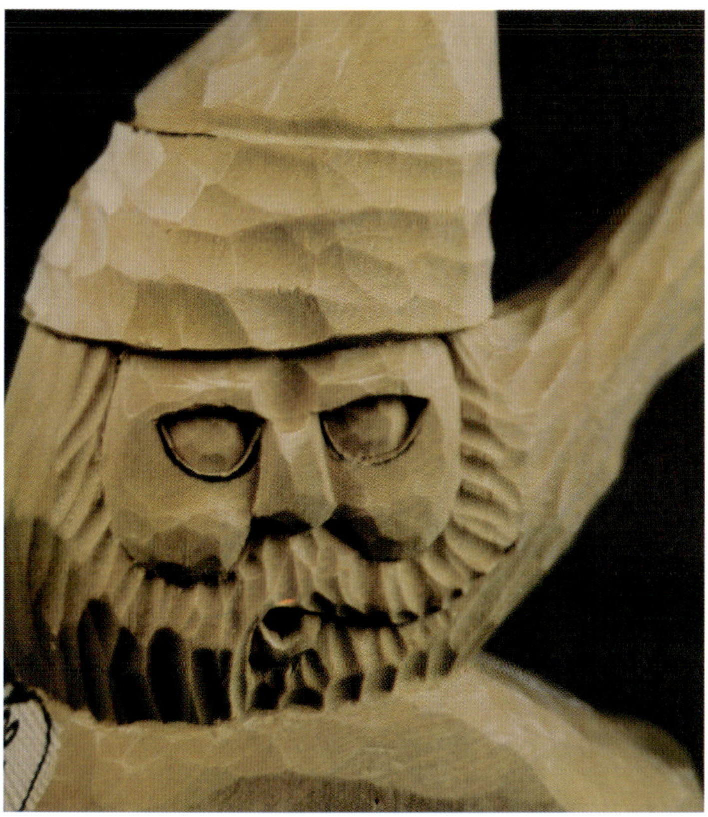

Add texture to the fur using the #9 6mm U-gouge.

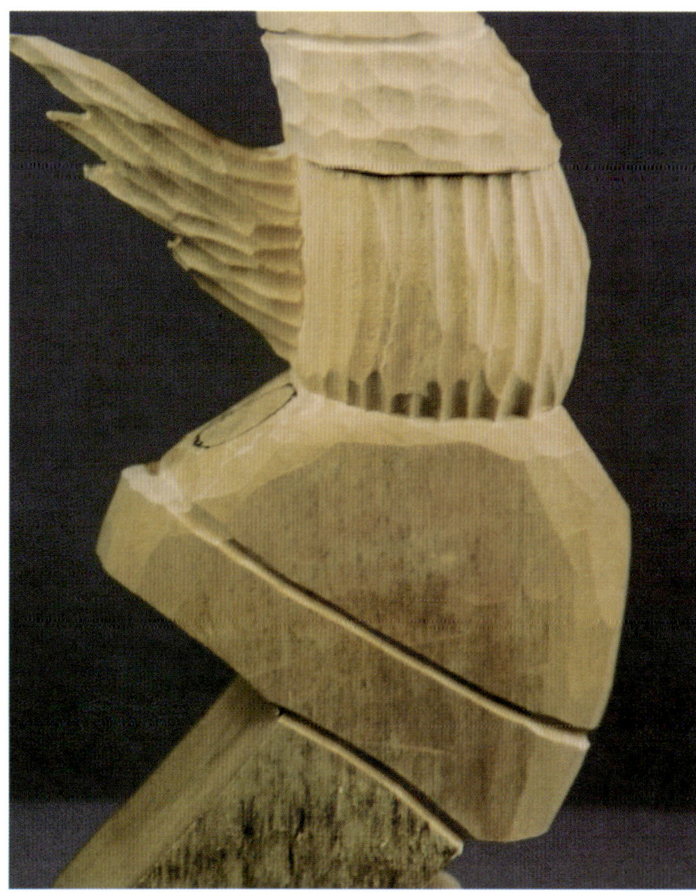

And in back. This V-groove separates the fur from the coat, and makes detailing it and painting it later a lot easier.

This completes the highest mountain we had to climb. Everything else is downhill from here!

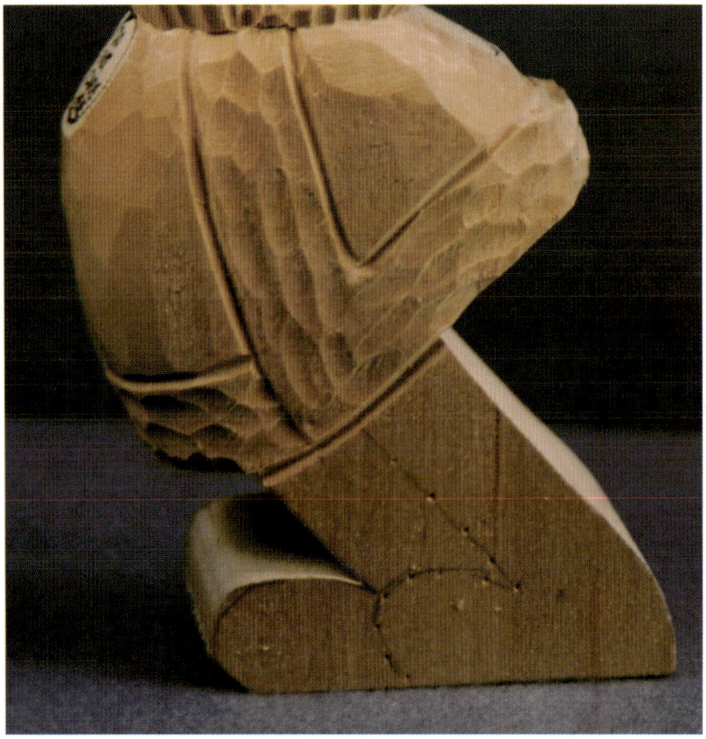

Use a #9 6mm U-gouge to add texture to the fur all the way around, as you did on the sleeves and hat earlier.

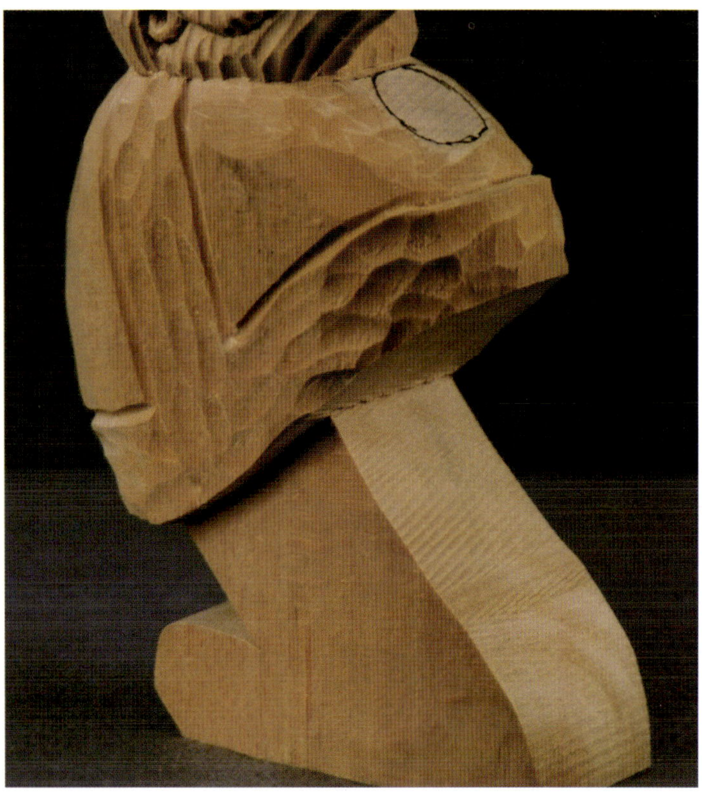

Incise below the fur at the bottom of the coat with your knife. Use your knife or #1 10mm straight gouge to remove wood all the way from the bottom of the feet to the top of the legs. Repeat as necessary until you have removed about 1/4" of thickness in front......

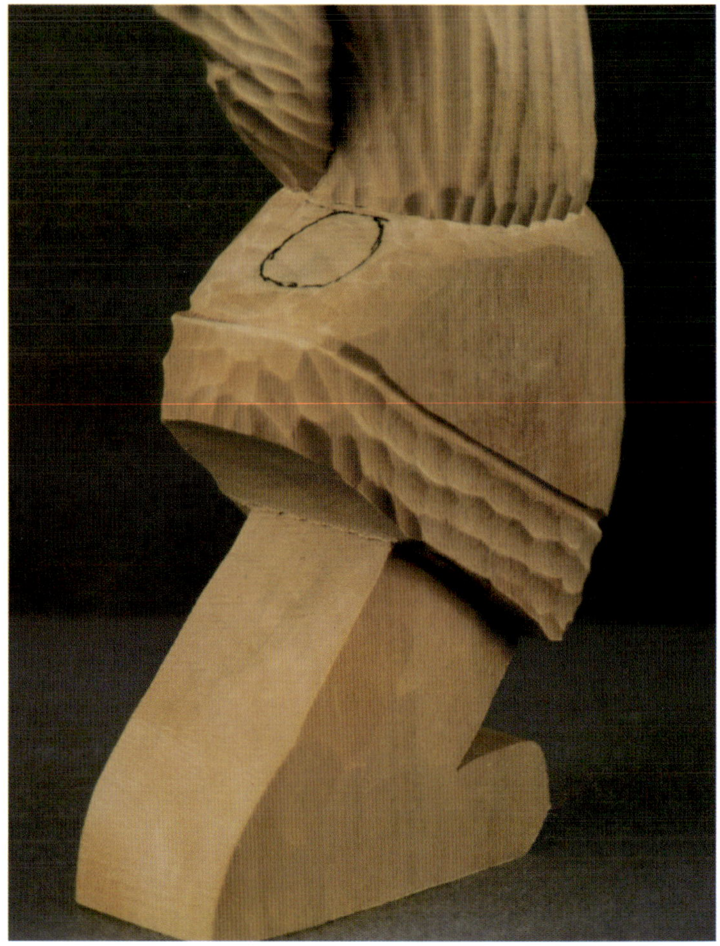

And in back.

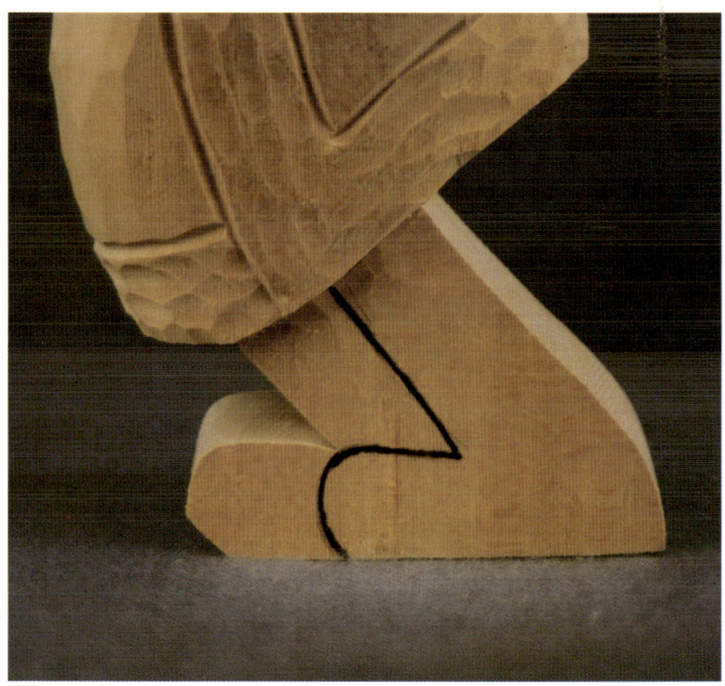

Sketch a line to define the legs and feet in front...

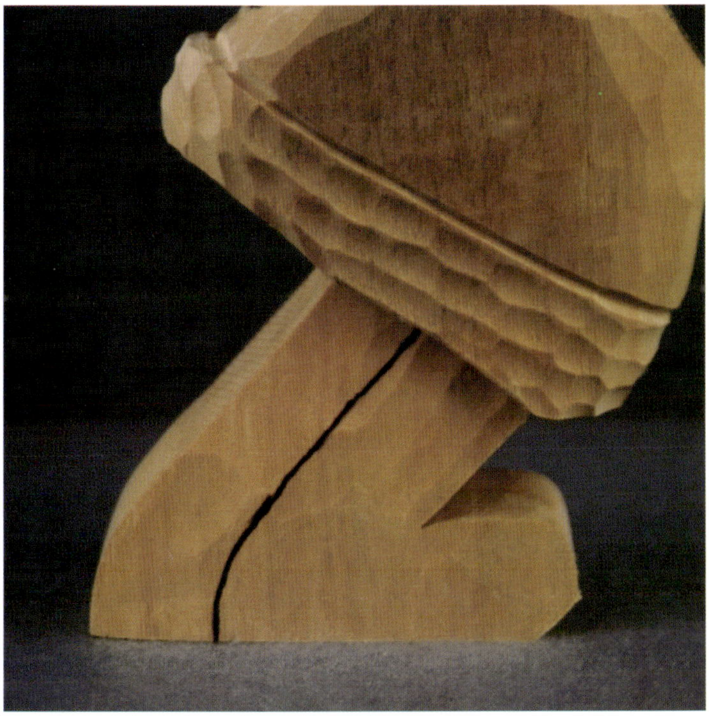

And in back.

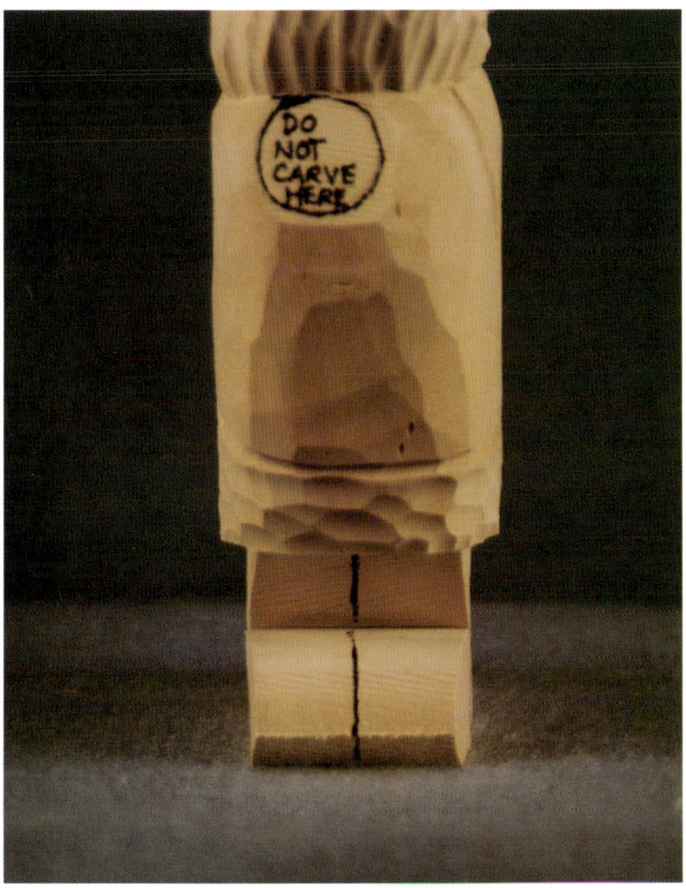

Sketch a centerline down the leg section to divide the left and right legs in front...

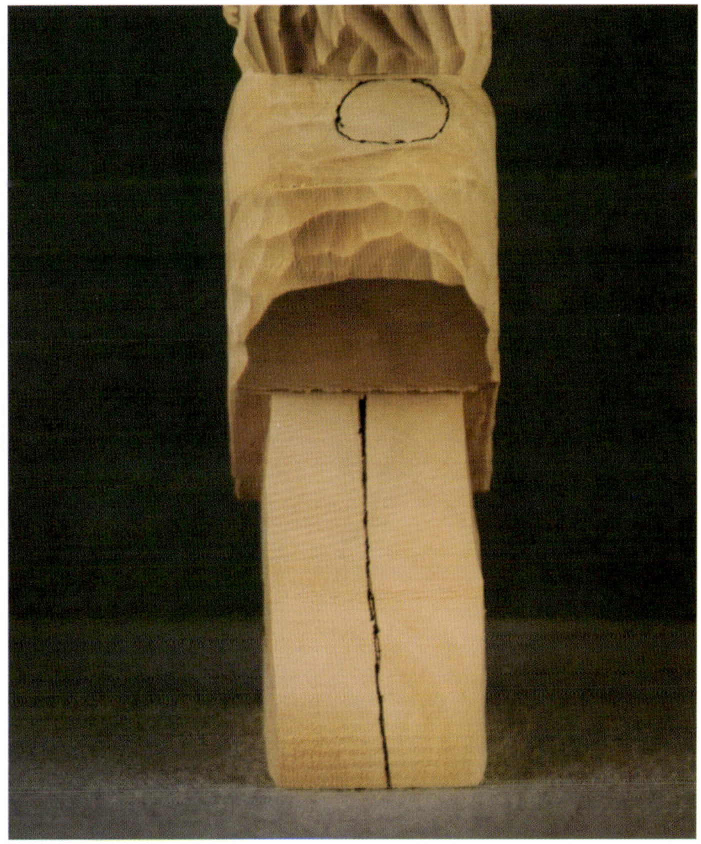

And in back.

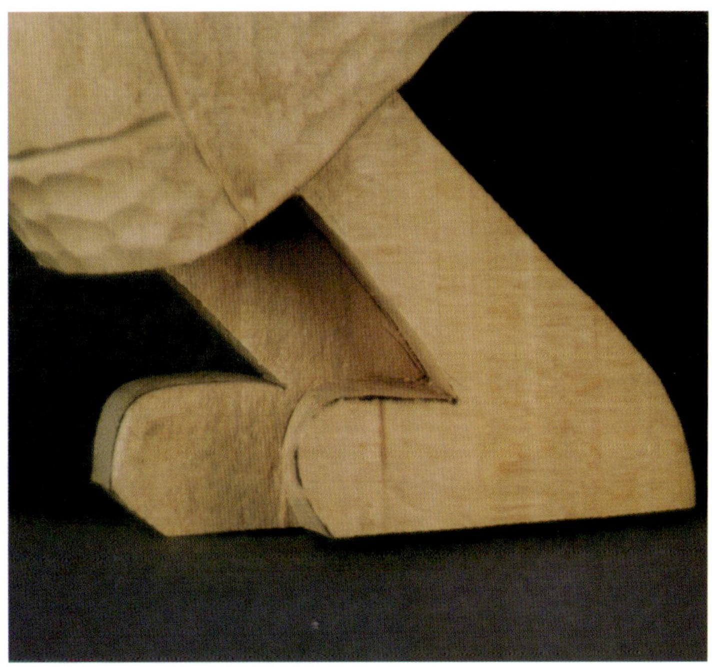

Use your knife to incise the line down the side of the leg section in front, and begin removing waste wood from the left leg, until you reach the centerline you drew earlier. Here is a front view of progress on one side.

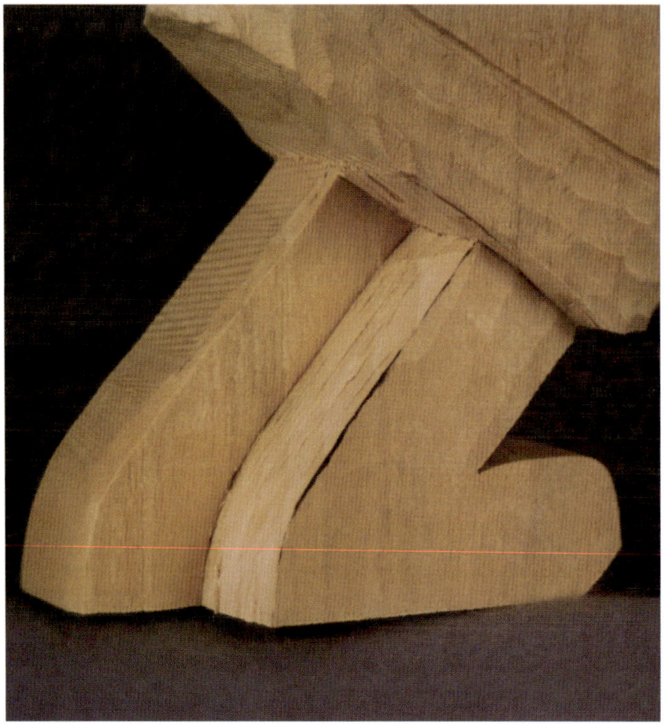

Repeat this process from the other side, paying careful attention to which leg and foot are in front of the other one. Here's how the other side looks so far...

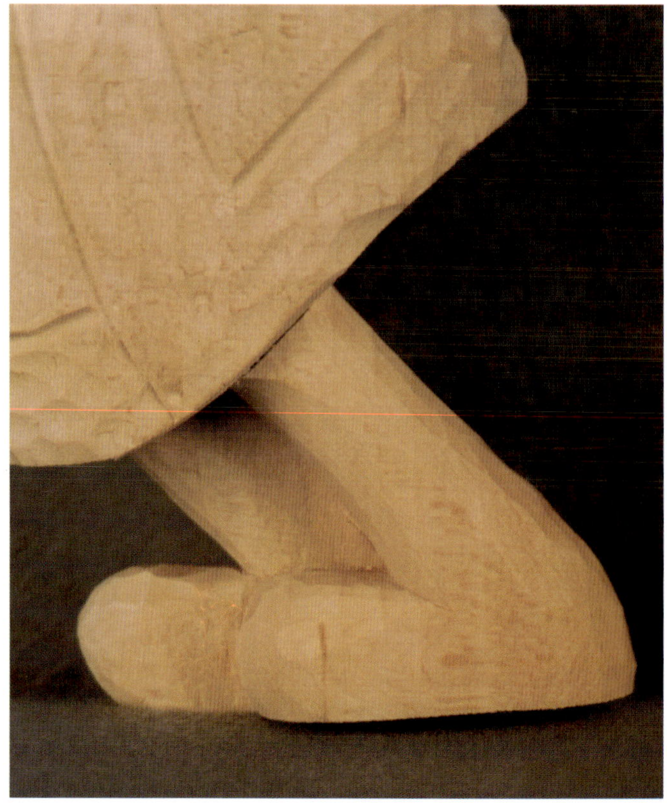

Using your knife, round off the toes and heels of the boots to reach this shape as seen from the side....

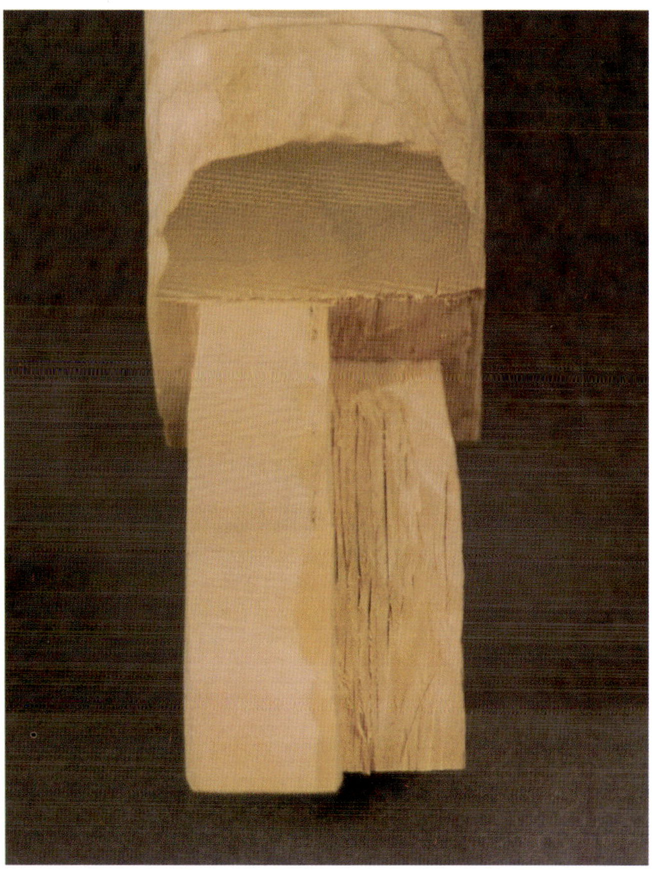

And here is a rear edge view so you can see another angle on the legs and feet, and how it should basically appear at this stage.

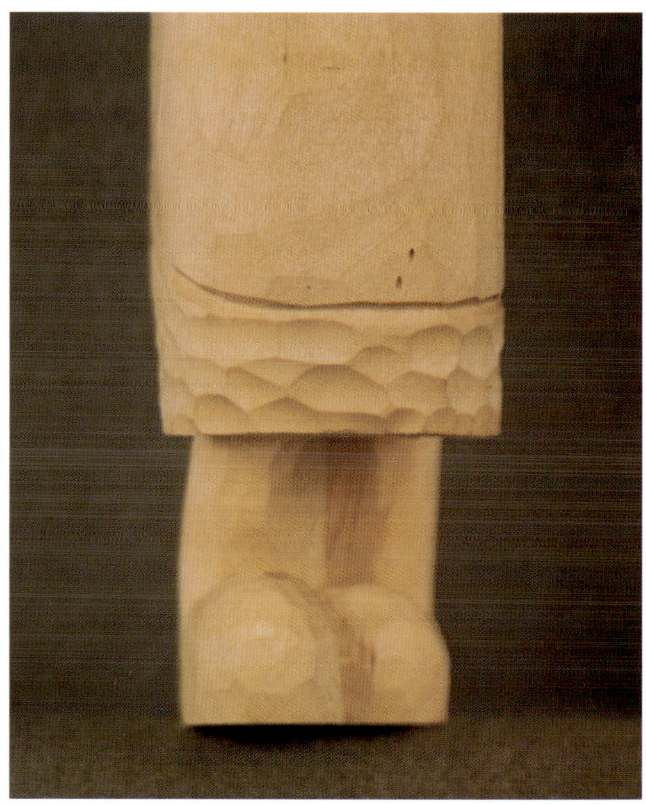

From the front...

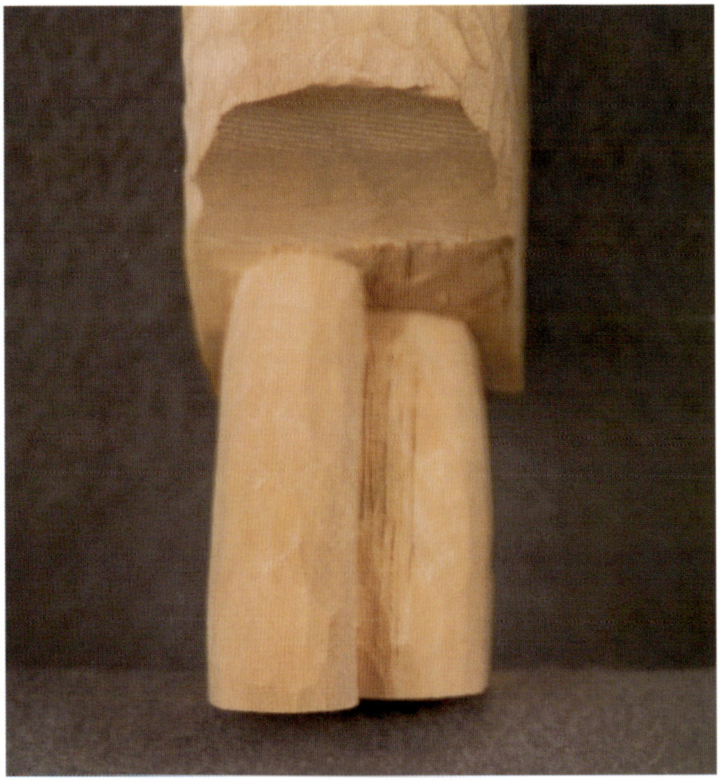

From the rear...

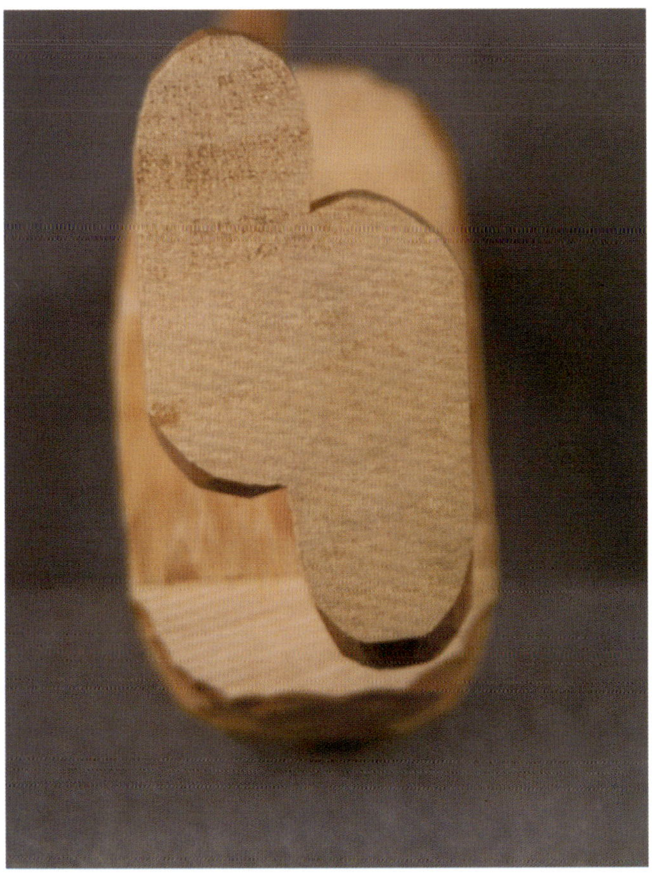

And from the bottom. **Note:** Your Santa may not be able to stand up now, but don't worry. We are going to mount and glue him to a base in later step of the project.

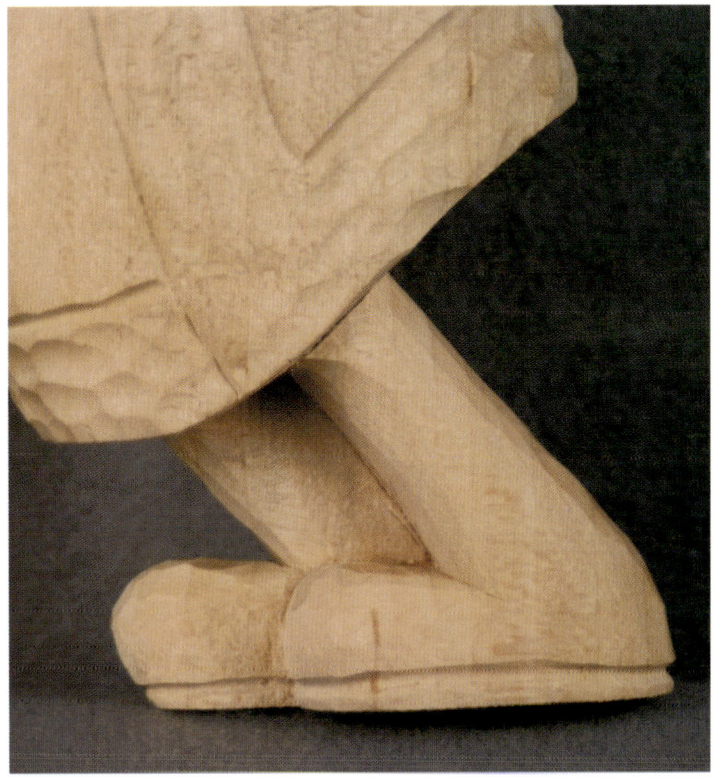

Use a #39 3mm V-gouge to cut a sole line all the way around the lower edge of the boots, as shown here.

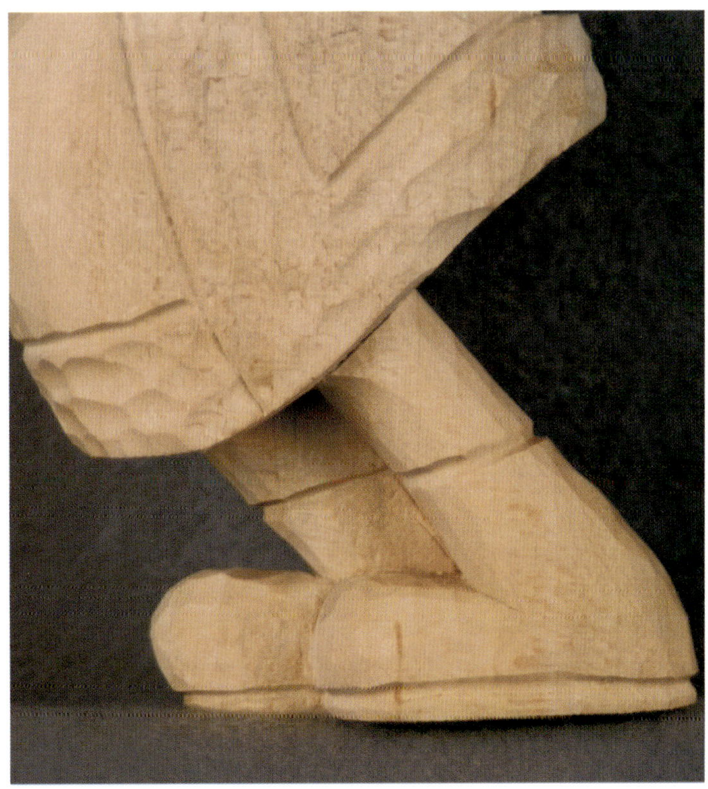

Sketch in the tops of the boots, and go over the lines with the #39 4.5mm V-gouge to separate the boots from the pants.

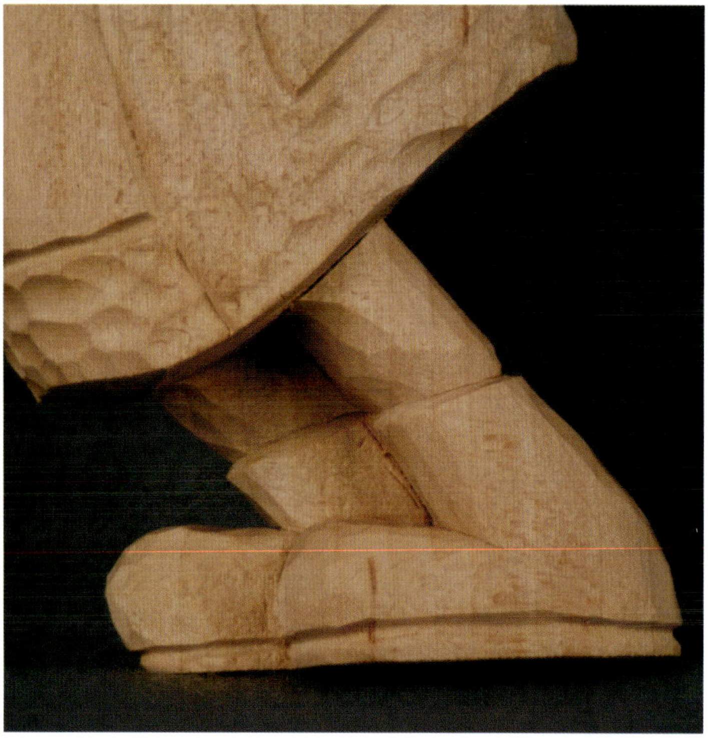

Shave down the legs, toward the tops of the boots, so that the pants appear to be going into the boots.

Well, if Santa had some arms, he would be dangerous. I guess it is about time to take care of that. Put a small spot of a good wood glue on one of the "no-carve" zones you were supposed to leave alone..you did leave them alone, didn't you? Using your finger tip, rub this glue into the wood to seal the area. *Stay inside the circle*, because the paint outside the circle won't be absorbed by the wood later if you have sealed it by spreading the glue too much. Do the same thing for the other "no-carve" zone, and also on the flat ends of both arms.

Clean your finger, and give the glue about 5 minutes to get into the pores of the wood and seal it, so you will get a super strong joint.

After about 5 minutes, put a small amount of glue on the flat end of one arm (it doesn't matter which one you start with), and gently spread it around. Clean your finger so you don't get any glue where it isn't supposed to be on the carving.

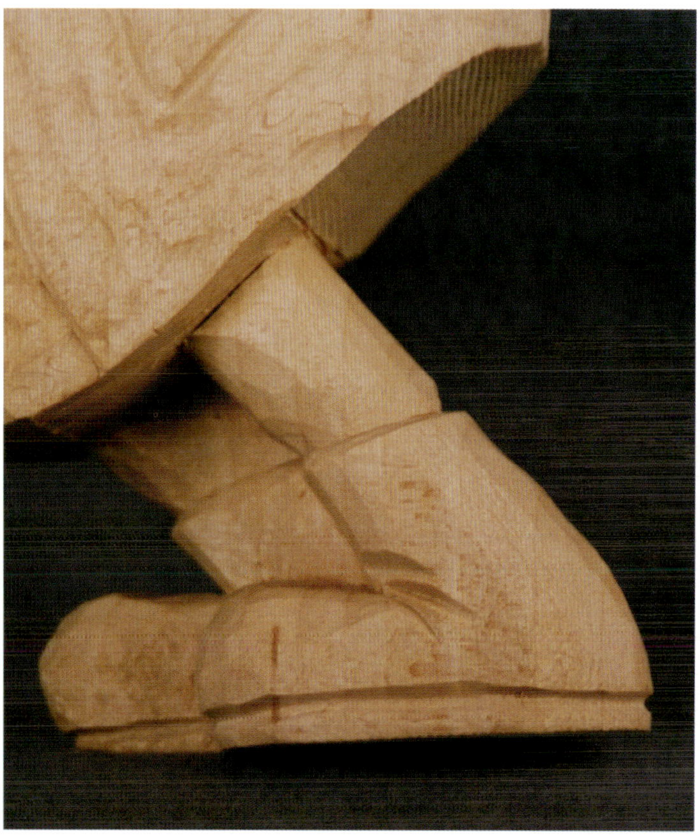

Last, use the #39 4.5mm V-gouge to cut in some "wrinkles" on the boots as shown. This just adds a little extra detail, and it won't hurt the carving at all if you omit this step.

Press the arm (with a fresh drop of glue applied to the end of the arm) against the body, centering it inside the "no-carve" zone. Be careful to glue the arm to the correct side of the body. If you get confused, look at your own hands and thumbs so you will be able to get the right arm where it should be, and the left arm where it should be. Keep pressure on the joint for about 30 seconds, then gently set the project aside so the glue can have about 30 minutes to set up. If any excess glue seeped out around the joint, use a small, damp paintbrush to clean it away, to prevent the glue from ruining your paint job later. After about 30 minutes, repeat the procedure for the other arm. Let the entire assembly dry for at least 8 hours. If you cheat and don't wait, I absolutely refuse to be put on a "guilt trip" because your glue joints failed. I know you're getting close to having a complete Santa, but after all this hard work, please give the glue a chance to do a good job for you.

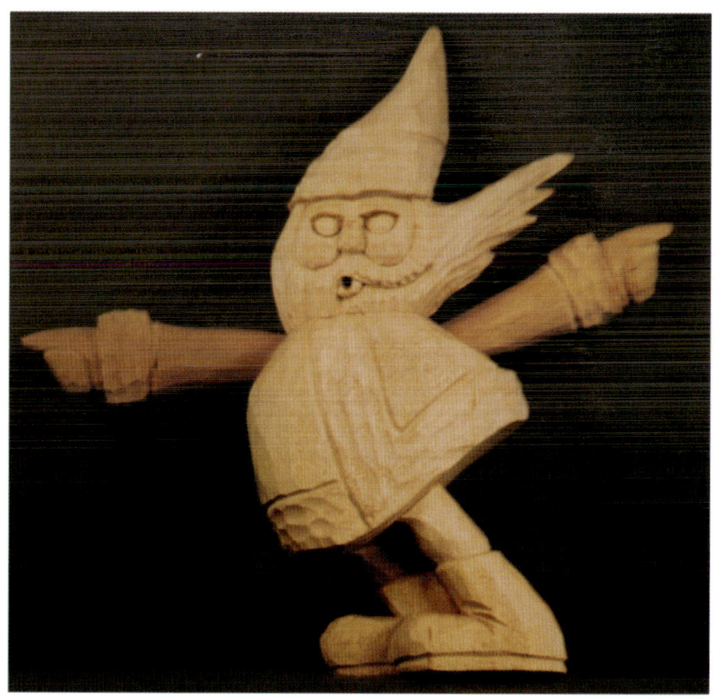

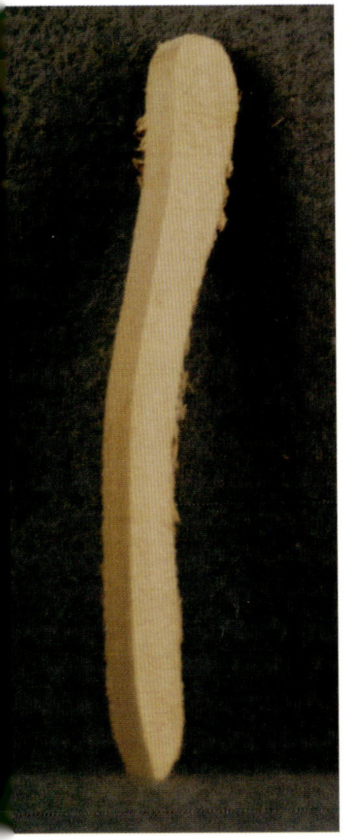

Transfer the walking stick pattern to a piece of scrap wood, and saw out the profile. Then, flip the wood over and saw out the profile again so you have it roughly shaped in all dimensions. You've got to do something while the arms dry, anyway. If you have access to small twigs, and would rather use a twig for more realism, go ahead and do it. Take a break while the rest of us carve a walking stick.

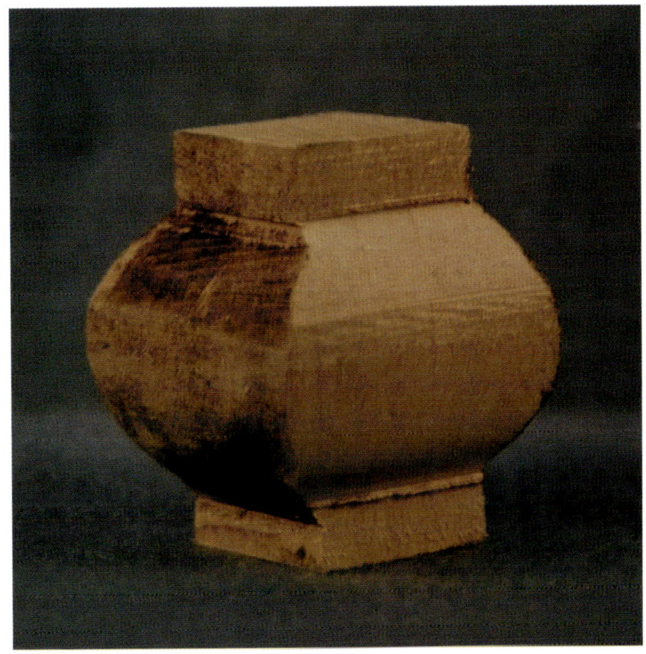

Transfer the lantern pattern to two adjacent sides of a square piece of scrap wood. (Cut the square piece of wood just slightly larger than the lantern pattern). Saw out the pattern on one side, but do not saw the wood completely away (yet). Make good partial cuts so you have the lantern fairly well defined. Next, flip the wood on its side, and saw out this profile completely. Then, turn the wood back on its original side and carefully finish sawing out the first profile, to arrive at this shape.

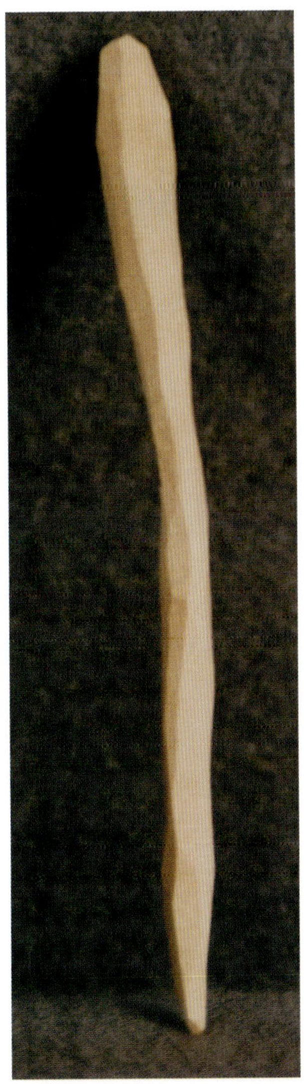

Use your knife to remove the sharp edges, applying the rounding techniques you are now an expert at using. Continue rounding and testing the stick in the hole in the right hand, until you get a good fit.

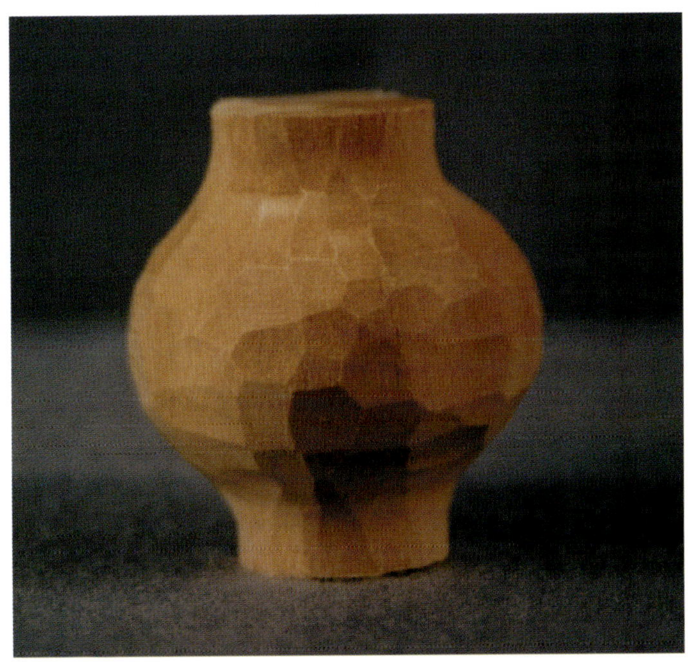

Being the experts that you now are, once more use your skills at rounding to remove the four sharp edges, then the eight newer sharp edges, etc., etc., until the lantern is rounded to your satisfaction.

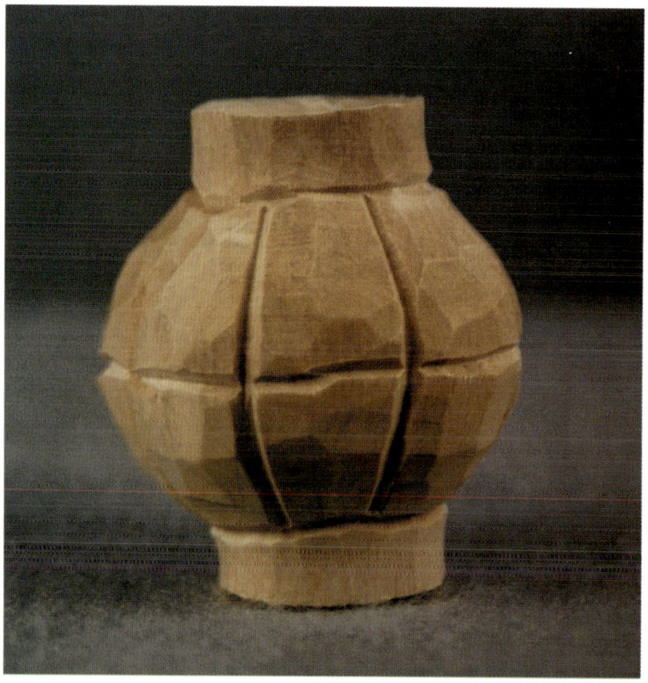

Now divide the lantern globe into eight equal sections, from top to bottom like orange slices. This is just an approximation,.... get the sections as equally divided as you can- I never use a ruler or compass. I'm not building a moon rocket, just a lantern. Besides, who's really gonna check you anyway? Trace over the lines with the #39 3mm V-gouge, then draw a horizontal line around the approximate middle of the globe (like the equator). Trace over this line, and around the top and bottom of the globe section with the #39 3mm V-gouge, and you now have a sixteen-section globe.

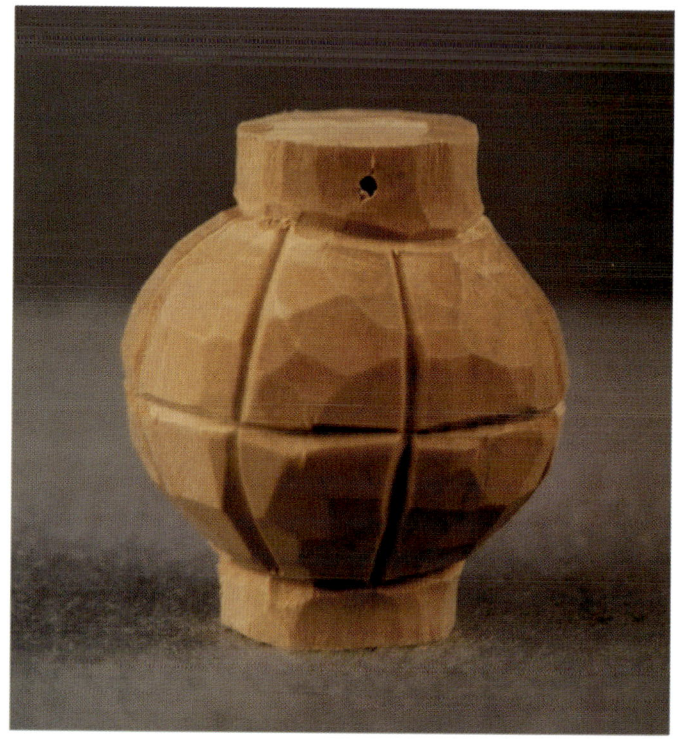

Last, drill a 1/16" hole through the top of the lantern, so we can put a wire handle through it later.

Guess what?!!....We're done with all the hard stuff. All that's left is to paint this guy, antique and varnish him, put the pieces together and glue him to the base for support. I normally go ahead and make the base before I start painting the carving. By doing that, the stain is dry on the base by the time I need to glue things to it. Using a piece of 3/4" thick pine shelving, or wood of your choice, saw it wide enough and long enough to give good support and stability to the finished carving. There are no exact dimensions here. The size of the carving will dictate the size of the base required, and that's about all I can say about that, and base dimensions in general.

Painting the Project

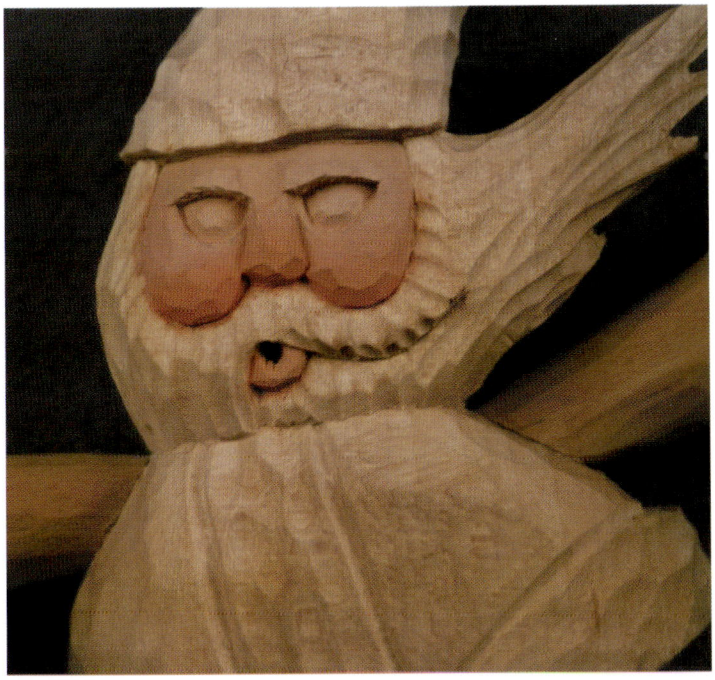

The face and lips are Fleshtone. After the Fleshtone is applied, while it is still slightly damp, blend a small amount of Blush Flesh into the cheek area, the tip of the nose, and the lip, to give a "windburned" effect.

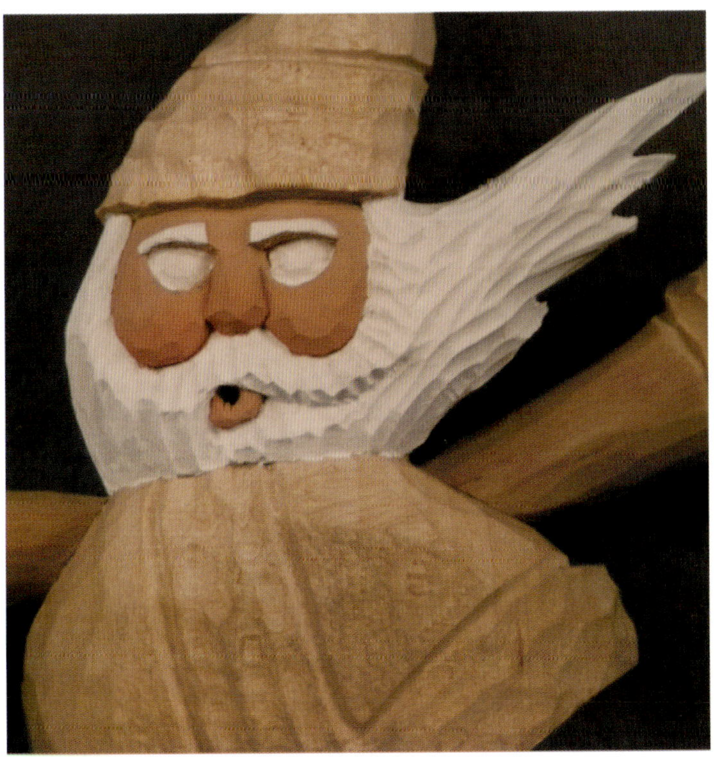

The eyeballs, eyebrows, hair, and beard are Titanium White.

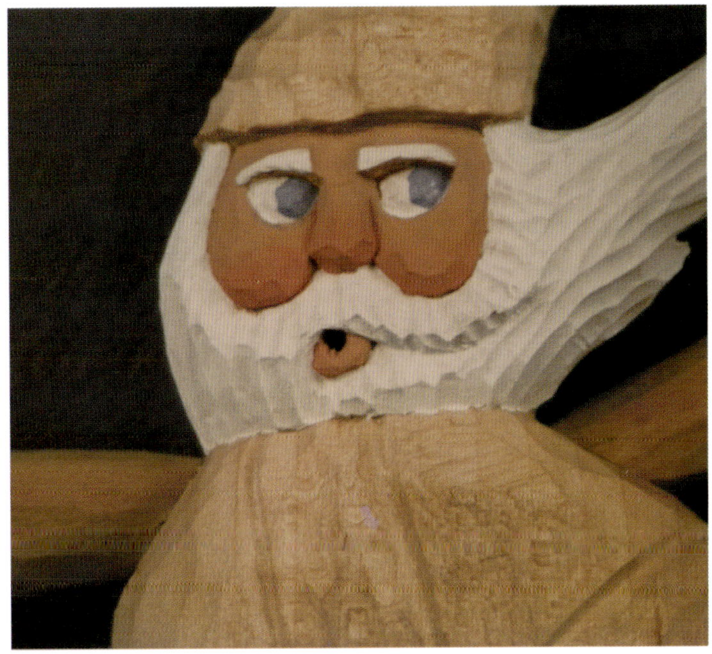

Once the eyeballs are dry, apply a dot of Baby Blue in the corners of the eyes, to give him the appearance of looking to one side.

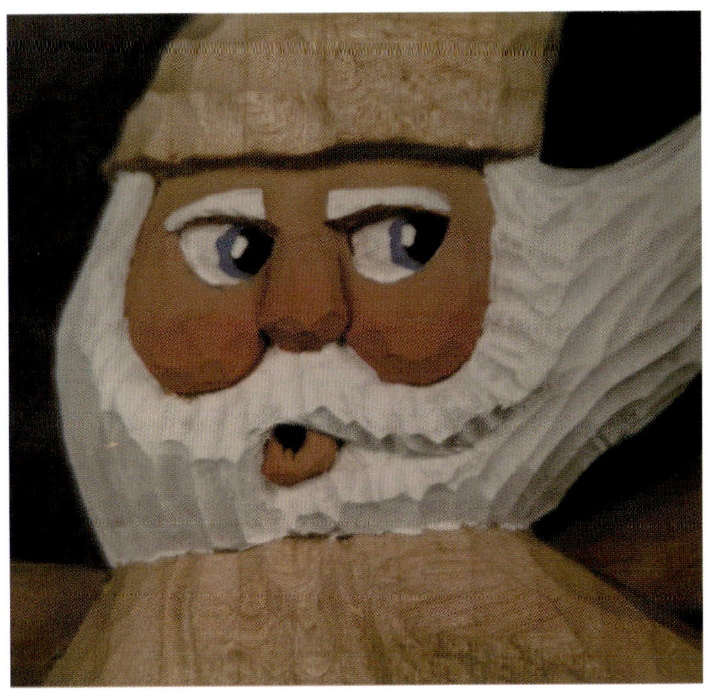

Next, put a dot of Lamp Black over a part of the Baby Blue. When it dries, add a tiny Titanium White "highlight" to give life to the eyes.

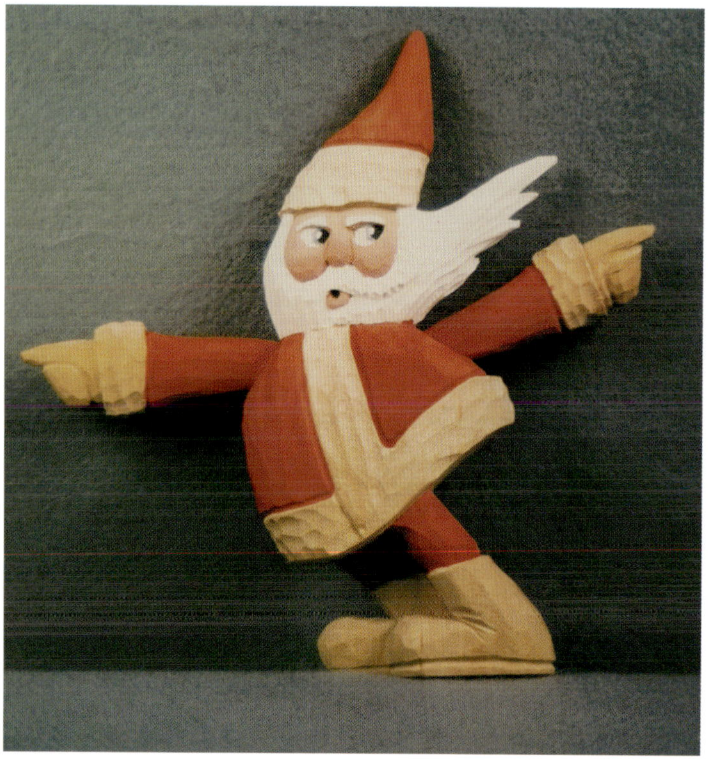

The hat, coat and pants are Santa Red.

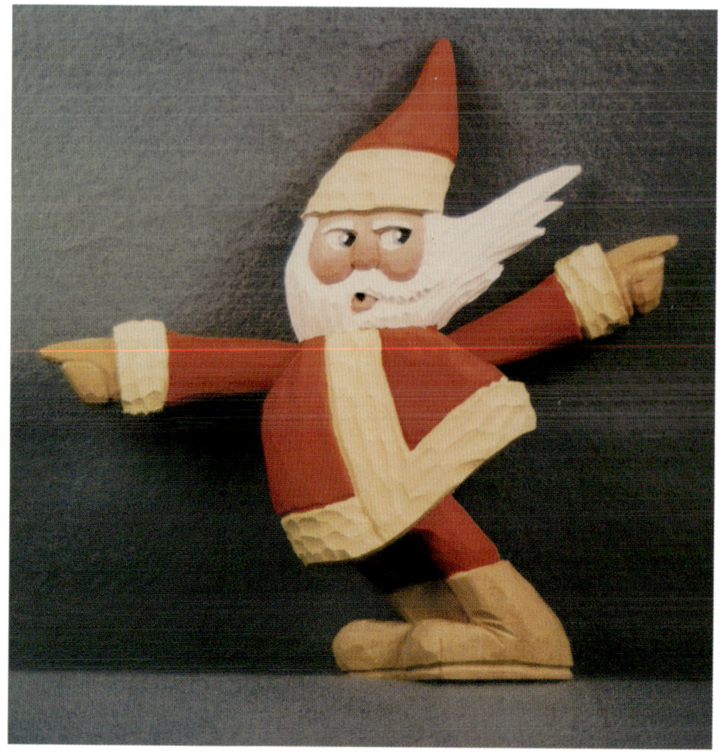

The mittens and boots are Lamp Black.

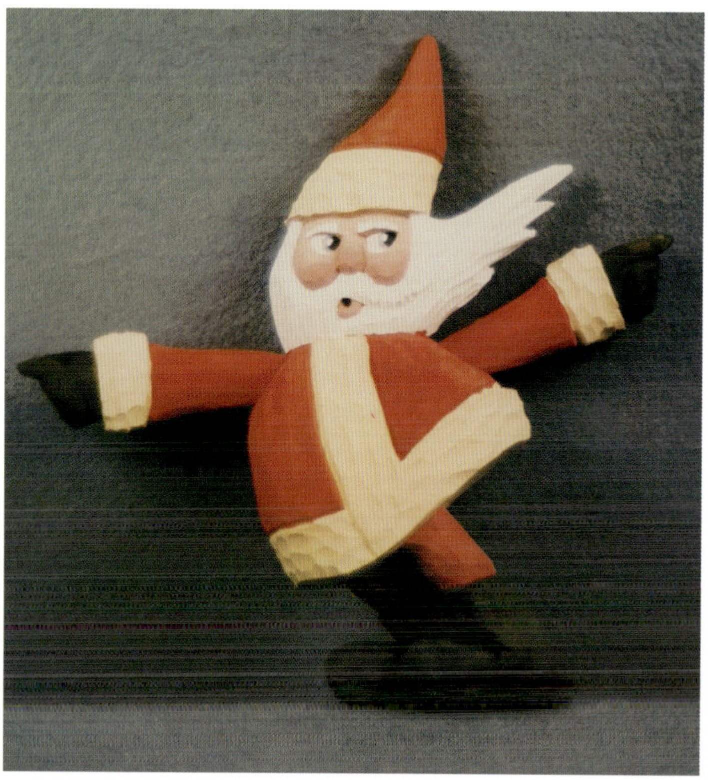

The fur is French Vanilla.

The walking stick is Burnt Sienna.

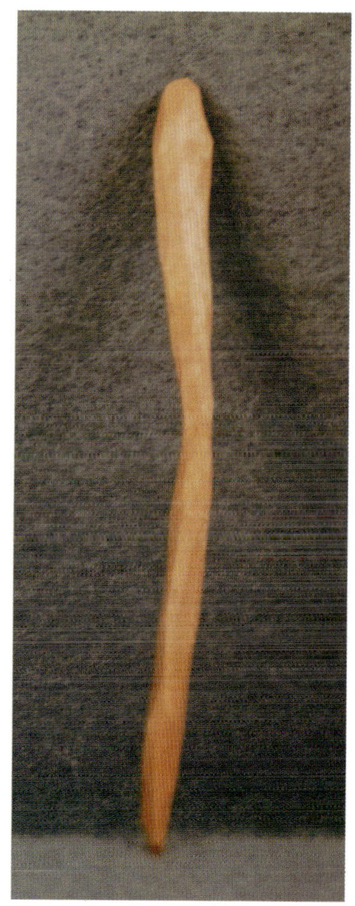

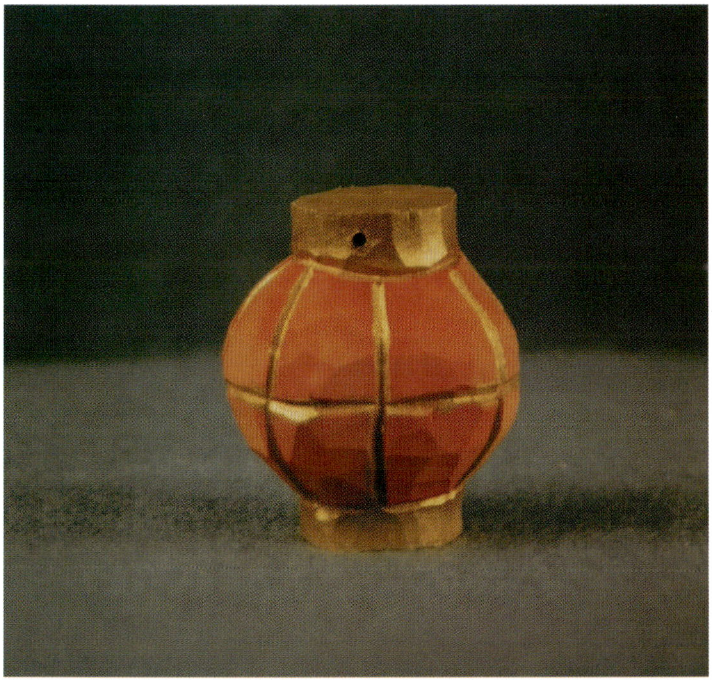

Paint the globe of the lantern Napthol Red. While the red is still damp, apply a small amount of Cadmium Yellow and blend it into the red to give a "glow" to the lantern. Then outline the globe sections and the top and bottom of the lantern with Venetian Gold.

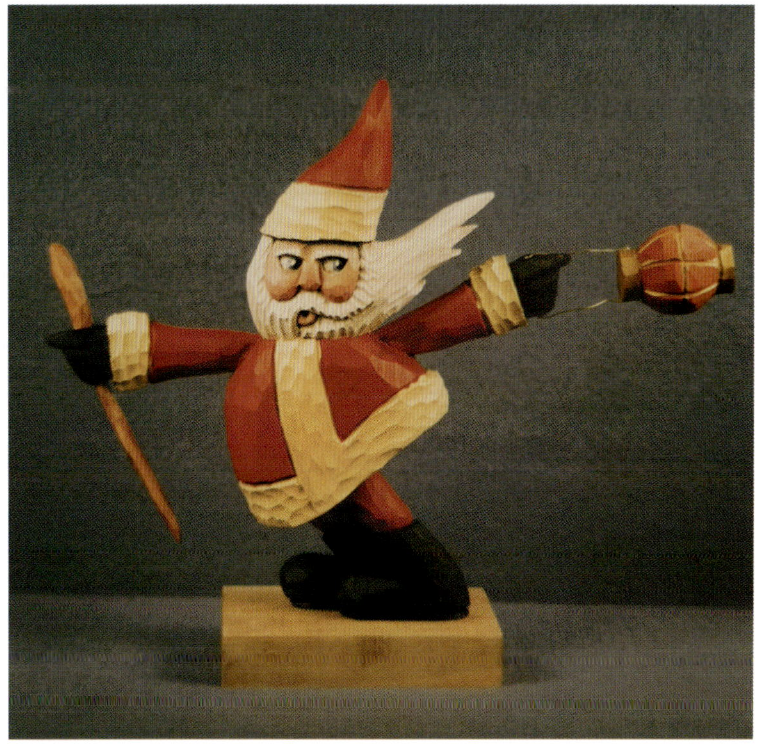

Front View.

Let the paint dry thoroughly. Apply the antiquing (such as Oak), and then seal the carving with the varnish (Clear Satin.... you just want a soft sheen, not to flat nor too shiny).

Apply a small amount of glue to the bottom of the feet, and rub it into the wood to seal it. This will help make a strong bond when attaching the body to the base. Once the glue has dried somewhat, apply some fresh glue to the bottom of the feet and press the body in place on the base. Hold it securely until the glue sets up, at least a minute or two. Let this assembly dry for several hours to become strong. Put a small dab of glue in the hole of the right hand, then slide the walking stick into position. If any excess glue comes out the bottom, clean it off with a small, damp paintbrush.

Next, take a small piece of wire, and bend one end at about a 90 degree angle. Insert it into the hole in one side of the lantern top. Then insert the free end of the wire through the hole in the left hand, and bend it back around, forming the lantern handle.

"Eyeball" where the wire meets the hole in the other side of the lantern top, then leaving about an extra 1/4", cut the wire. Bend the free end at about a 90 degree angle, and insert it into the hole. This may take one or two trial-and-error passes, or you might get lucky the first time.

We are now through, and I'll bet your project looks great! I've included some photos of the finished project for your reference.

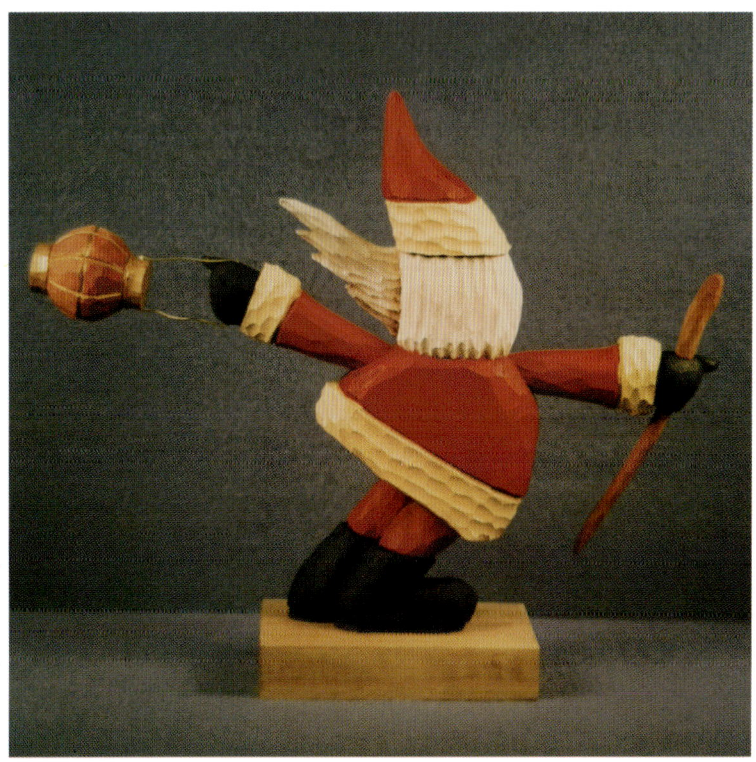

Rear View.

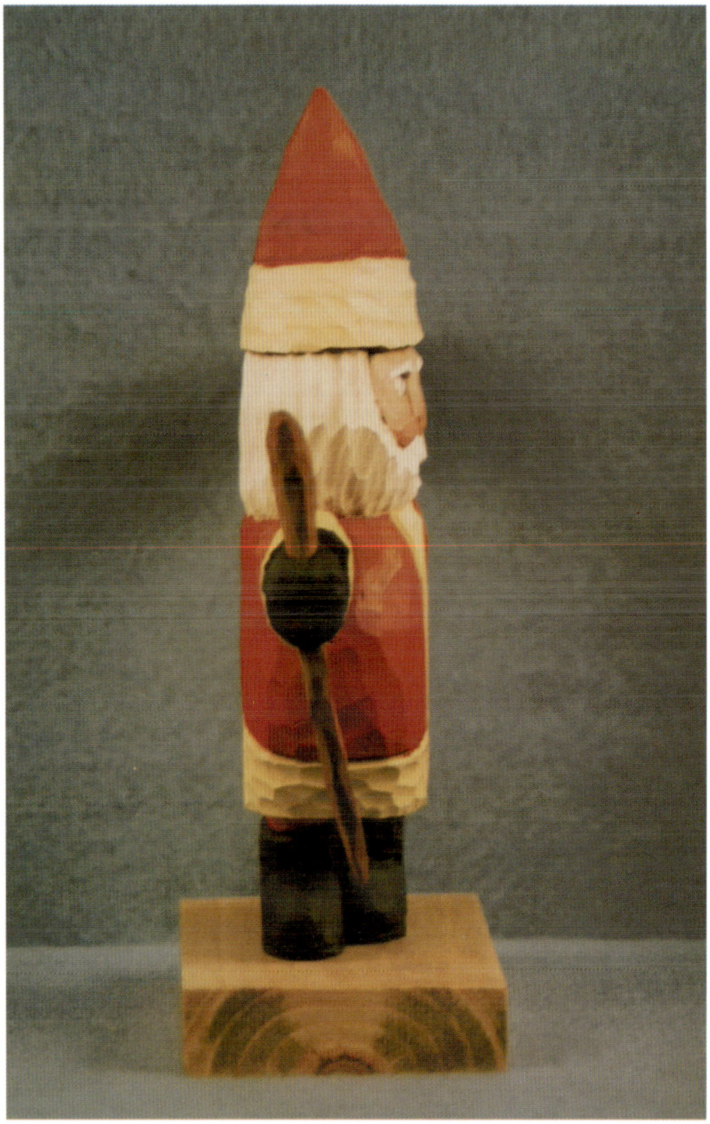

Side view from front.

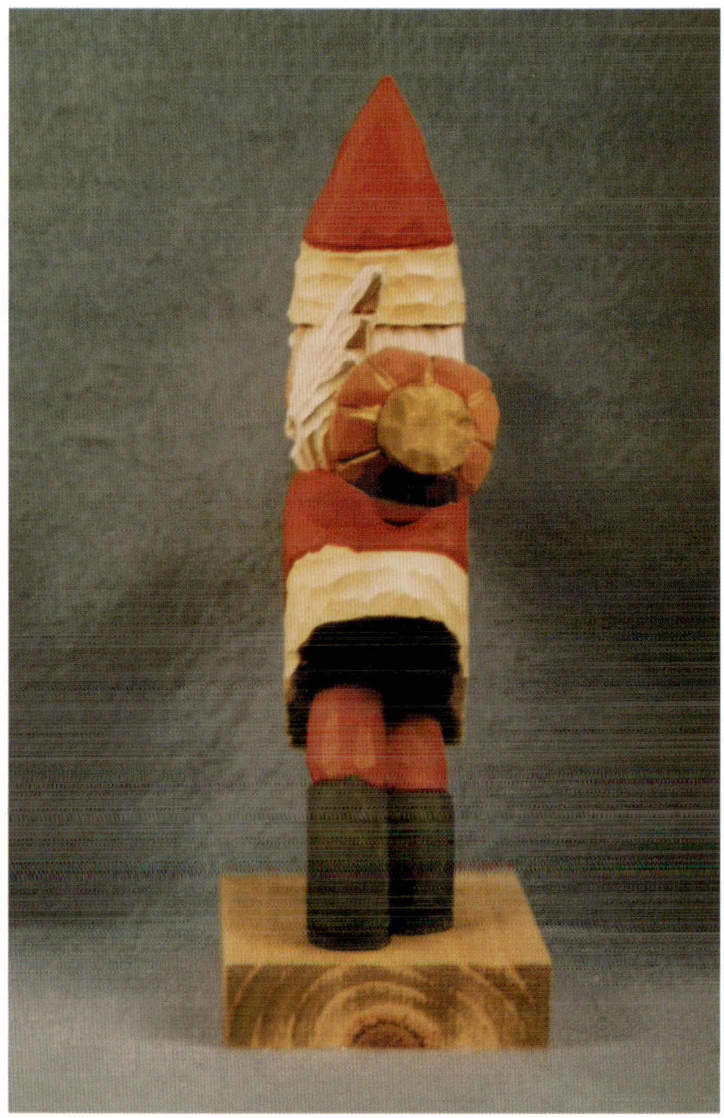

Side view from rear.

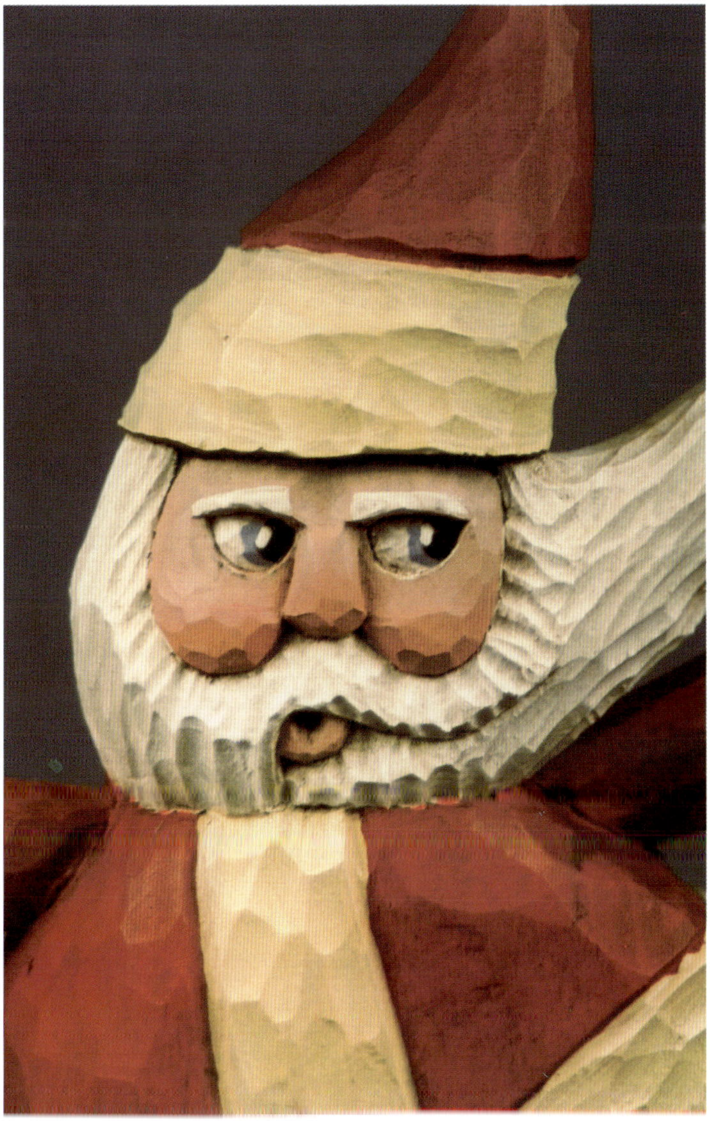

Close-up of face.

For future posterity, you should sign, number and date your carving. This makes it more valuable to the collectors who will be seeking out your work some day, if not already. I hope that in some way I have been able to help each of you with some aspect of carving and painting. When we share tips and information, we all become better. If you have any comments or questions about something in this book, or if you have an idea you'd like to see me put in a future book, please feel free to write , e-mail or call me at the following address and telephone number. I welcome any comments or suggestions you have.

Gallery and Study Models

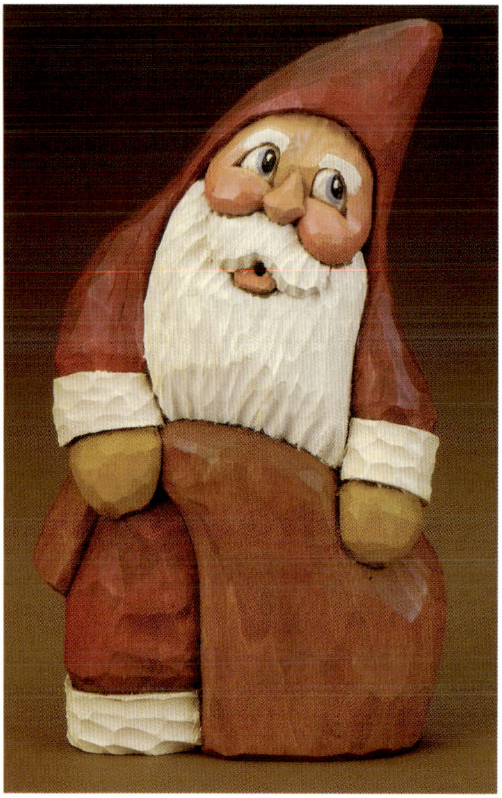

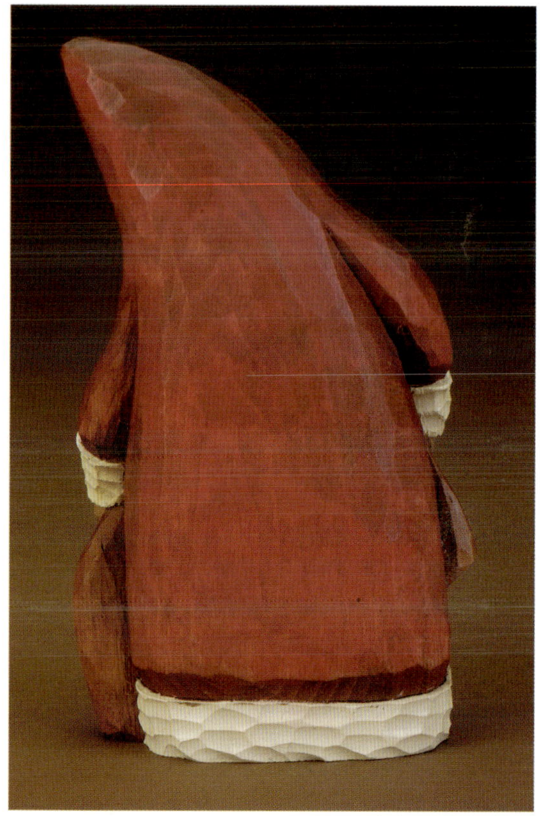

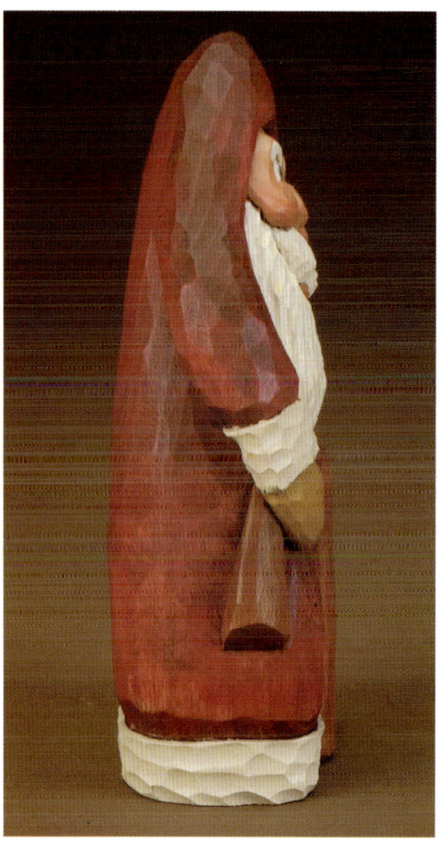

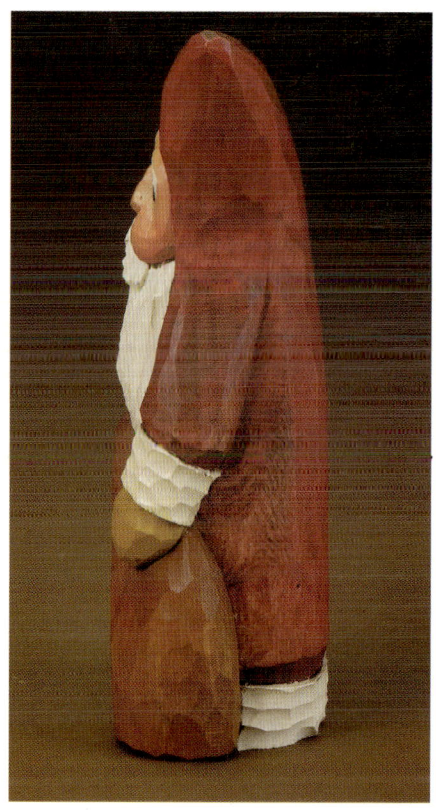

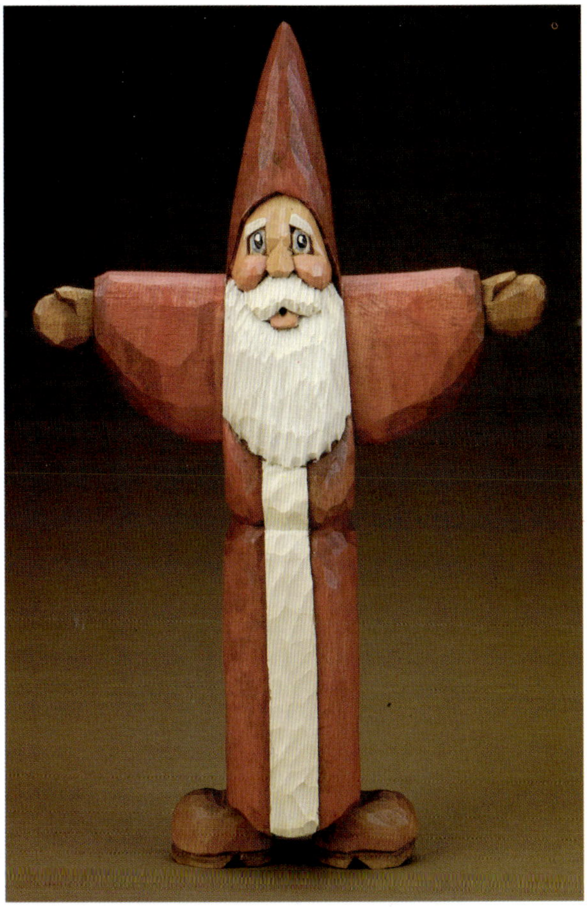

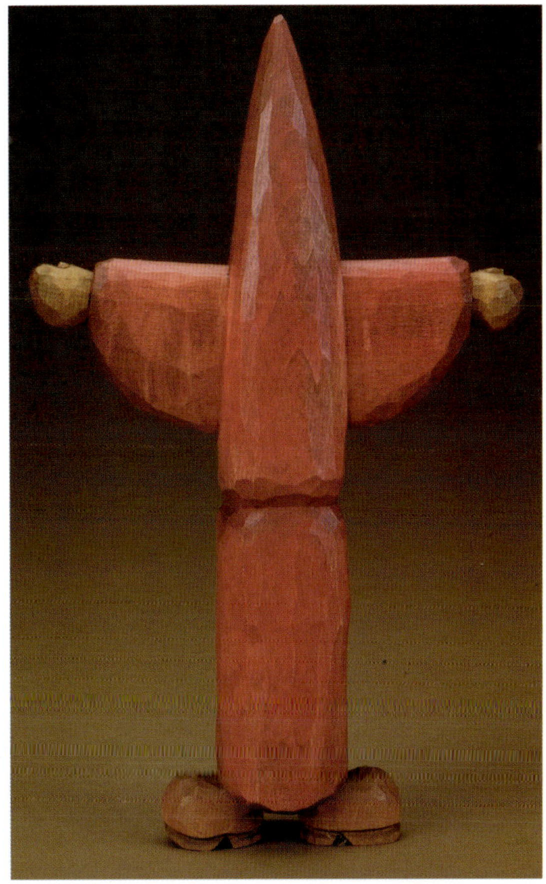

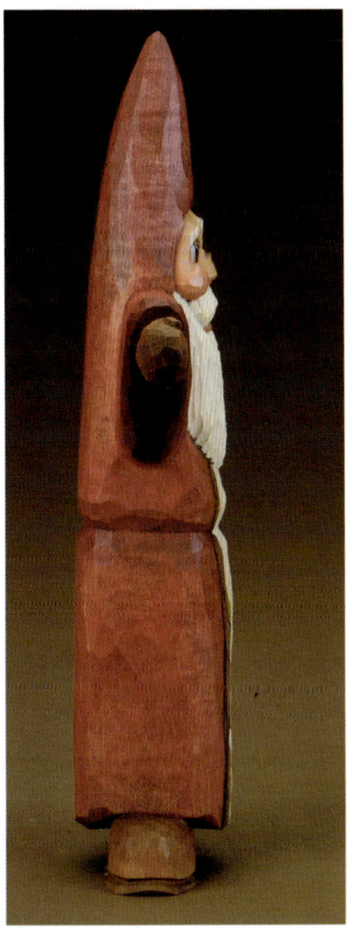

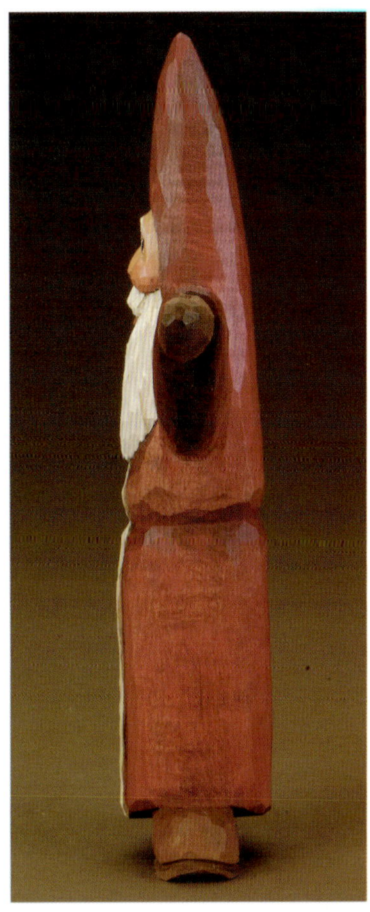

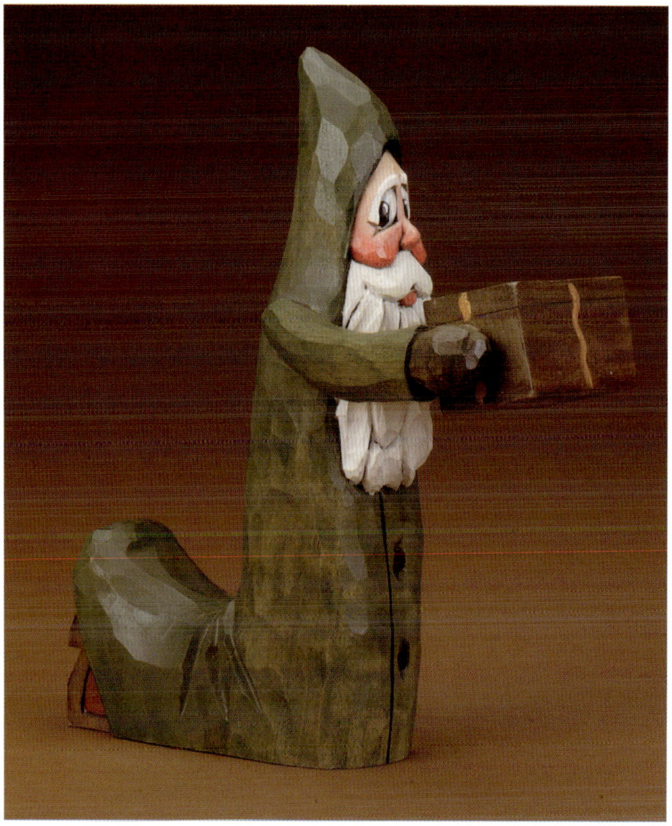

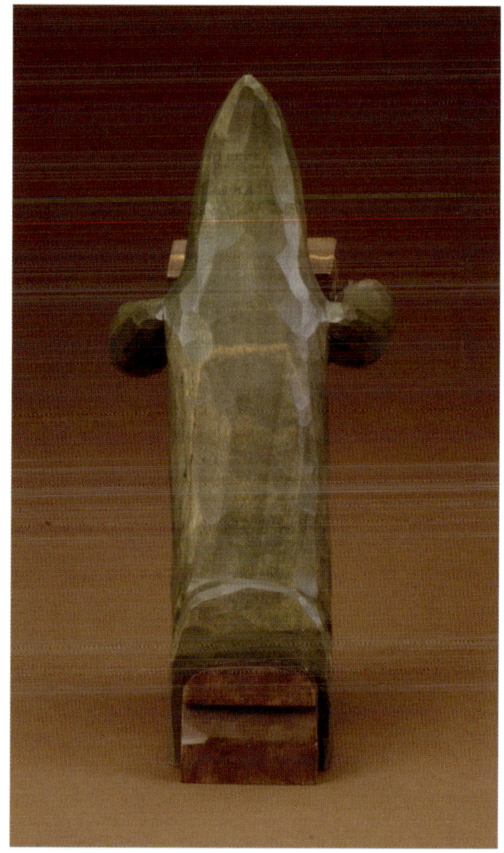

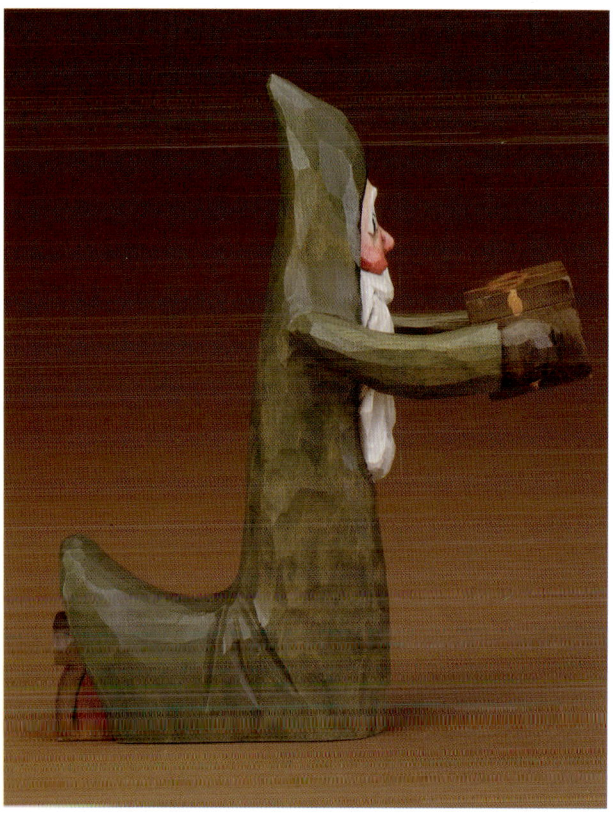

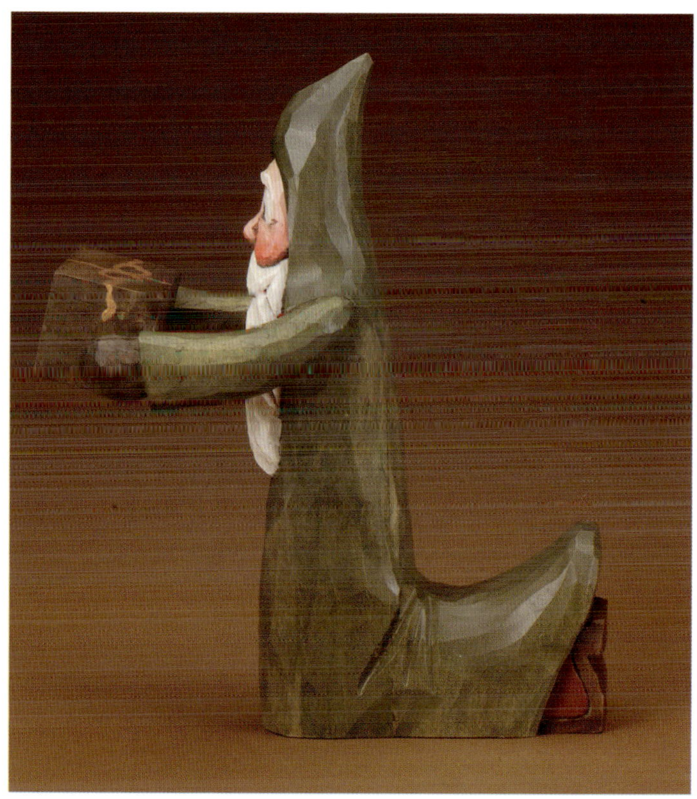

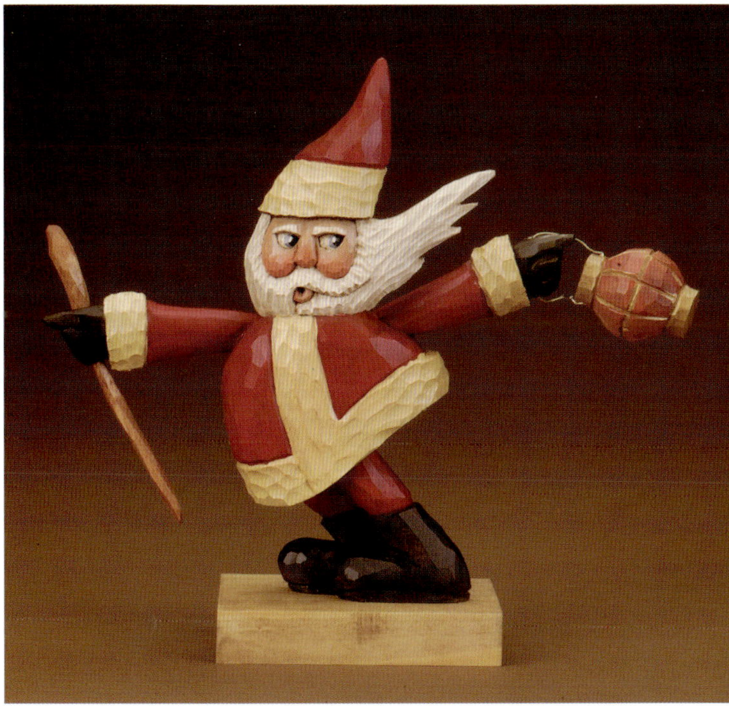

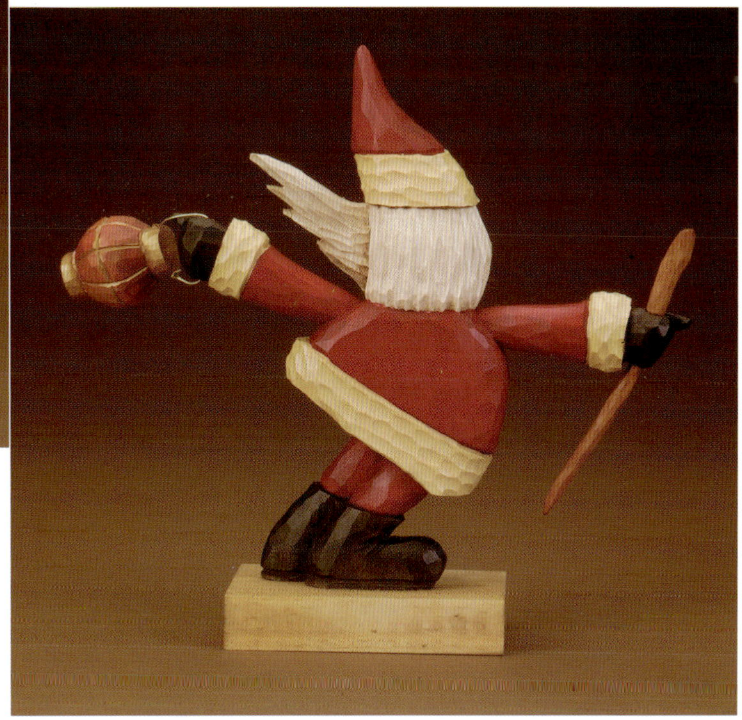

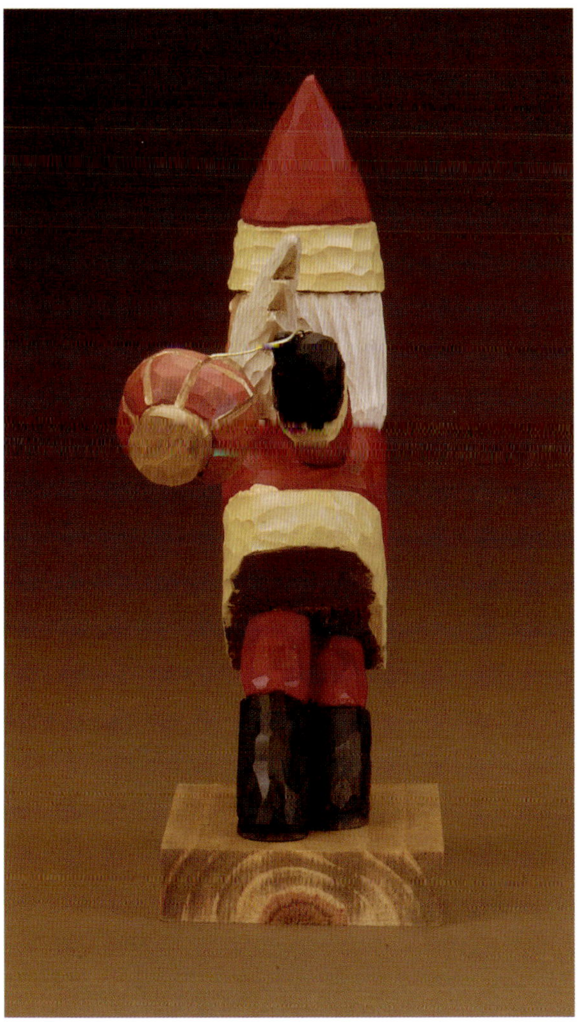

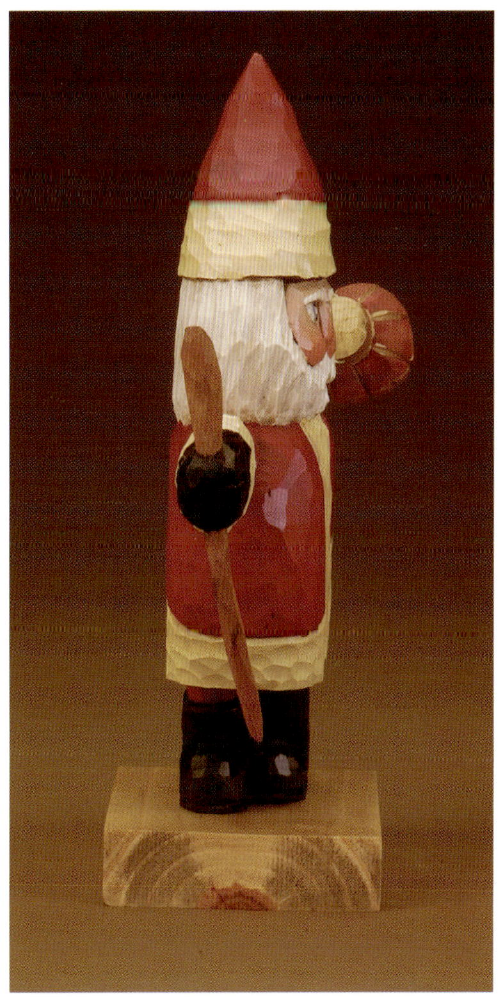

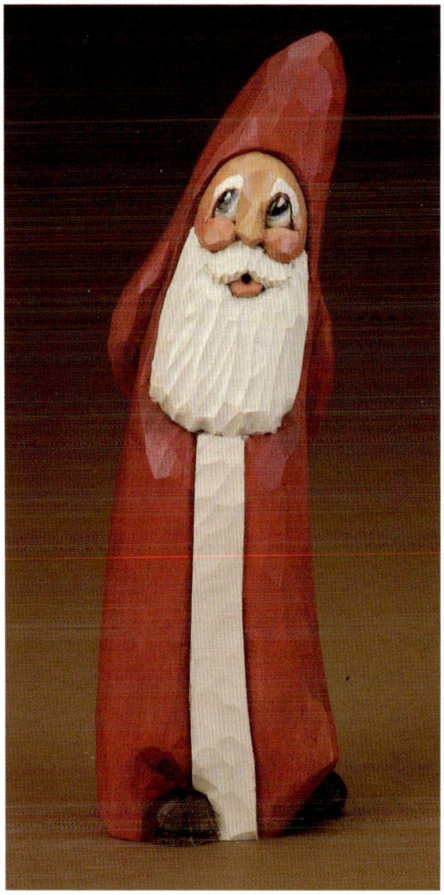
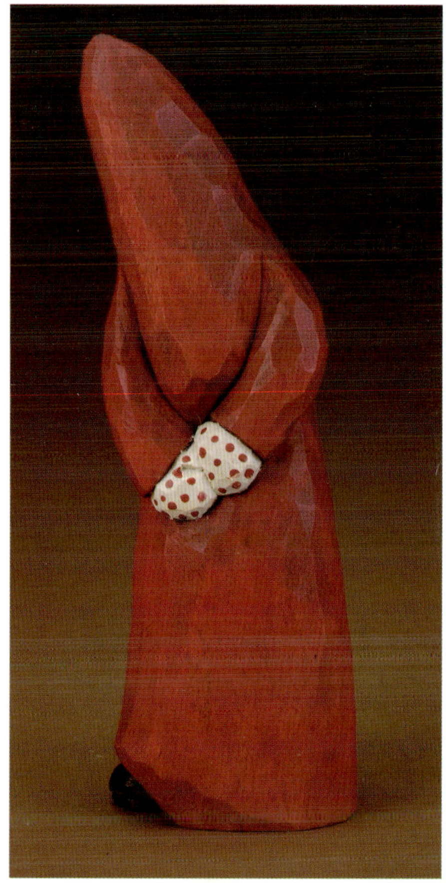
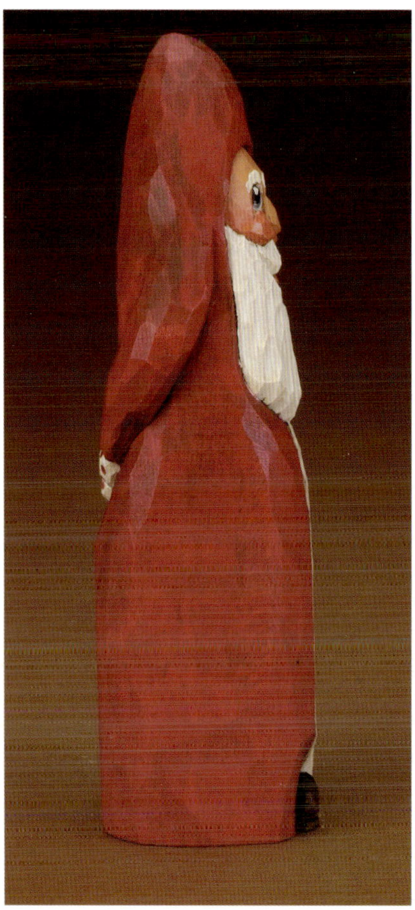
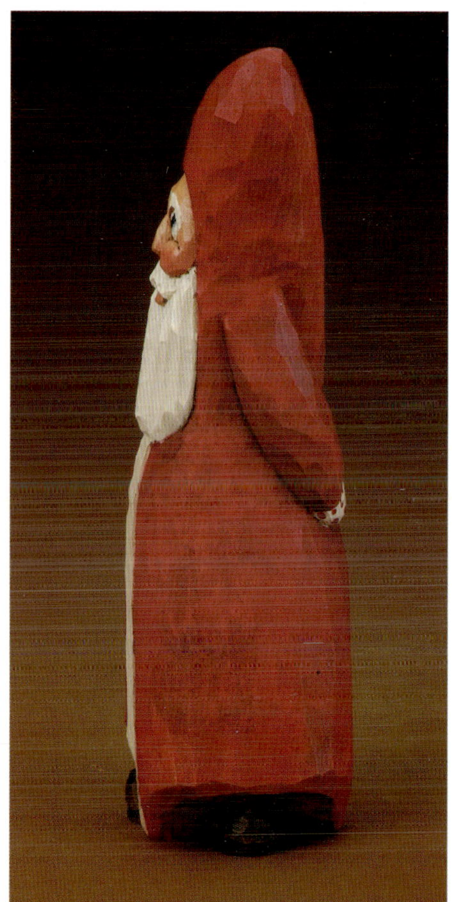